I0812049

Jim Henson's™ LABYRINTH™

VHS | VISUAL HANDBOOK SERIES

Jim Henson's™

LABYRINTH™

The Making of Jim Henson's Iconic Film

Paula M. Block & Terry J. Erdmann

INSIGHT EDITIONS

SAN RAFAEL • LOS ANGELES • LONDON

Contents

OPPOSITE Brian Froud's early conceptual painting of the Four Guards.
ABOVE TOP Sarah is unmoved by Jareth's emotional entreaties.
ABOVE BOTTOM Hoggle and Sarah standing on a ledge above the Bog of Eternal Stench.

Chapter One

"Once Upon a Time"

On June 27, 1986, Jim Henson jotted down a brief entry in the Red Book, a personal log he'd kept since 1965: "*Labyrinth* opens in the US."[1]

Despite this succinct sentence, *Labyrinth*'s debut was important. If this ambitious film—the tale of a teenage girl who takes a heroic journey into the heart of a maze to save her baby brother from goblins—were successful, it would allow Henson to further expand his vision to create increasingly elaborate and thematically complex feature films. While *Labyrinth* was in production, he said to Mary Manilla, the PR director for Henson Associates, "I want the film to be successful enough that I can do another one."[2]

Though *Labyrinth*'s theatrical opening did not deliver the way Henson was hoping for. Initially deemed an interesting "also-ran" in a summer crowded with blockbusters, the film placed eighth during its opening week on US box office charts. But amazingly, that is not the end of its story.

Over the four decades since its premiere, *Labyrinth* has experienced a fascinating reversal of fortune. Today, the film is recognized as a wildly imaginative, fancifully inventive coming-of-age allegory. Its ardent admirers are legion, particularly those who came of age with the film. A perceptual change has taken place: In the same way that the character Sarah learns there is an opening in the wall if she looks at it the right way, perception has changed the way people see *Labyrinth*.

Jim Henson's son Brian, now chairman of the Jim Henson Company, thinks the audience's initial response had a lot to do with their preconceptions. "People who were fans of my father didn't know how to respond to it," he says. "And people who were fans of David Bowie's didn't know how to respond to it."

Despite these challenges, *Labyrinth* was—and still is—a magnificent demonstration of "old-school" filmmaking. It relied primarily on matte paintings, masterful puppetry, animatronics, and in-camera visuals: Jim Henson created visual tricks with very few postproduction visual effects. Every participant, in front of or behind the camera, gave their all to make *Labyrinth* an amazing piece of entertainment—and they're still proud of that work today. At the time, nothing even remotely like it had appeared on the big screen—and no one has attempted such a feat since.

LEFT A random bevy of beasts in one of Brian Froud's early sketches. **ABOVE** (left to right) Pages from one of Jim Henson's ever-present sketchbooks, detailing a rough sketch of Hoggle and the inspiration for the Nipper Sticks and the initial thoughts on what to call his new project and a sketch of the labyrinth itself.

The seed that eventually grew into *Labyrinth* sprouted in the back seat of a limousine in December 1982. Present were Jim Henson, British fantasy illustrator Brian Froud, and Brian's wife, the sculptor and puppet-maker Wendy Froud. The trio had just attended a San Francisco screening of Henson's all-puppet feature film opus *The Dark Crystal*. The mood in the limo was mellow, if a bit weary. "We were all so tired after making *Dark Crystal*," Brian recalls. "We'd said, 'Never again!'" So it came as a bit of a surprise to Brian when, from out of nowhere, Jim posed a question. Should they make another movie?

Brian was briefly dumbfounded—but only briefly. Even though *The Dark Crystal* had just opened, he realized that Jim Henson's creative mind, never content to linger too long on one project, was already anticipating future opportunities. Brian and Wendy had enjoyed collaborating with Jim on *The Dark Crystal*. In fact, during production, the couple had met, fallen in love, and gotten married. It didn't take long for them to consider Jim's question. "We just said, 'Oh, yes!'" Brian relates. "But he had no idea of what he wanted to do."

So the trio began to brainstorm, moving from one idea to the next, when Brian mentioned goblins, a topic he was familiar with. "And Jim's eyes just lit up," says Brian, "because he could understand goblins."

Several of the details the trio tossed around in the limo endured throughout the lengthy writing process of the script. For instance, Brian suggested placing the film's action within a labyrinth, a location ripe with metaphorical exploration. "I don't know where the idea came from," he admits. "It just seemed to me that labyrinths have a mysterious depth, and that there are symbolic things that go on underneath. So it wasn't just a physical place, but also a mental state with a lot of symbolism to it. And Jim said, 'Oh, yeah—that's great.' And we left it at that!"

Henson provided one caveat. This time around, he said, "I want people in the film." That turned out to be a real game changer, explains Brian: "One of the reasons that *Dark Crystal* is still a classic is that it's all puppetry. That's why it will always stand out in history. So when Jim said we'd put people in it, I wasn't really sure what that meant. But what I eventually came to realize was that when you've got puppets, especially in strange circumstances, that the human beings could vicariously put life into the puppets as well."

He adds, "And suddenly this vision of a baby surrounded by goblins came into my head. I thought it would touch people's

PREVIOUS SPREAD "My concept paintings helped shape the story of the labyrinth; some of the characters were written in, some were not," said Brian Froud. These finely dressed musical goblins did not make it into the script. **RIGHT** Battle-ready goblins.

hearts when they saw something that's seemingly threatened but is utterly relaxed and actually a part of that strange world. And when Jim said, 'Okay—what's the story?' I immediately said, 'Well, goblins traditionally steal babies. That's dramatic. That's in Grimms' fairy tales." Henson liked it. A short time later, Brian returned to England, where he painted the first piece of art for the film: a beautiful laughing baby surrounded by ugly goblins.

The writing process eventually took more than two years and involved a variety of "helping hands" before Henson felt that it was ready to shoot. In essence, Henson kept reworking the screenplay until it embodied the emotional tone he was searching for. In *Labyrinth*, Henson wanted to create something magical and visually transformative—with a very human heart. He said the story was about the "growing-up process of maturity, working with the idea of a young girl right at that point between girl and woman, shedding her childhood thoughts for adult thoughts. Specifically . . . the idea of taking responsibility for one's life—which is one of the neat realizations a teenager experiences—a central thought of the film."[3]

Labyrinth was the latest and most ambitious in a succession of goals that Henson had been setting for himself since his teen years.

The Potential with Puppets

"I was seventeen years old when I first started building puppets and working on television," Henson said in 1986. "For a long time, it was just something to do to go through college, paying my way through school. Then, very slowly, I realized that this was something that a grown man could do for a living."[4]

Starting in 1969, Henson's increasingly popular puppets were an integral part of PBS's *Sesame Street.* The Muppets then became the stars of their own television series, *The Muppet Show,* which ran from 1976 to 1981. The Muppets also starred in several TV movies, and in 1979, Henson made a successful leap to the big screen with *The Muppet Movie.* All this proved that the potential of the Muppets was sky-high. But Henson wanted to challenge himself artistically, so he decided to try something radically different. In 1982, this resulted in the motion picture *The Dark Crystal,* a groundbreaking labor of love. All this success fed his hunger to expand the scope and complexity of puppetry and to create thematically satisfying storytelling that appealed to both children and adults. This desire to keep innovating led to the television show *Fraggle Rock,* which ran from 1983 to 1987, the 1984 movie *The Muppets Take Manhattan,* and then to his cinematic return to fantasy in 1986 with *Labyrinth.*

"Puppetry is one of the oldest theater forms," Jim Henson stated while working on *Labyrinth.* "It's been around as long as theater has. It's an ancient tradition that draws on myth and legend. I feel I'm part of that tradition in using several of these elements and old techniques, but I enjoy converting them to the worlds of film and television."[5]

This ancient tradition brought him together with the man who would become an executive producer on *Labyrinth*: George Lucas. "While we were making *Star Wars* in England," said Lucas, "we worked across the street from Elstree Studios, where Jim Henson's group was taping *The Muppet Show,* and I got to know him. I really admired the Muppets, so I asked Jim if he thought we could get together and create a very realistic-looking puppet."[6]

The puppet Lucas was alluding to was Yoda, who debuted in *Star Wars: Episode V The Empire Strikes Back* (1980) and who became an integral part of the *Star Wars* universe. Although Henson didn't participate directly on *Star Wars,* he introduced Lucas to puppet designer Wendy Froud (then known by her maiden name,

PREVIOUS SPREAD A youthful Jim Henson breathes life into an early creation. **RIGHT** When creating *Labyrinth,* Jim Henson posed a rhetorical question about the film to its imagined audience: "Is it all a dream, like *Alice's Adventures in Wonderland,* or Dorothy's in *The Wizard of Oz*? It's whatever you like to make it. Wherever it takes you to."

Midener), who was working on *The Muppet Show*. Wendy would later sculpt the character of Yoda from Stuart Freeborn's design. Henson also introduced Lucas to longtime Henson puppeteer Frank Oz, who performed the character. This fruitful relationship led, four years later, to Lucas joining the team that produced *Labyrinth*.

Lisa Henson—who is the oldest of Jim and Jane Henson's children and today is the CEO of the Jim Henson Company—remembers the period when her father was developing *Labyrinth*. "He was disappointed in the Gelflings' [lack of] expressiveness in *Dark Crystal*," she says. "He thought, 'If you want something to look like a human, you should probably cast a human.' Bernie Brillstein [Henson's longtime friend and agent] and the producers/advisors in his life felt that it had been a hard sell to do a movie with puppets only. If he could combine the best of puppetry and animatronics techniques with movie stars or performers, it might potentially be more commercial, and there wouldn't be a struggle with the 'expressiveness' of the humanoid characters."

Lisa continues: "I remember him talking about the combination of actors and puppets, and trying to achieve the right sort of reality, where they could 'live' together. You had that in the Muppet movies, of course, but the Muppets are idiosyncratic—they don't fit in the human world, yet you just accept them."

For *Labyrinth*, she says, "He really wanted this new fantasy movie to have kind of a seamless reality. The humans and creatures should fit in together."

"Our puppets had a quality that people really responded to," observes Brian Froud, who designed all the creatures for *Labyrinth* and *The Dark Crystal*. "The trick of all of them is that you somehow recognize either something of yourself or something of the world in them."

In part, *Labyrinth* was another creative exploration of the age-old craft of storytelling. "It is a wonderful stretching exercise," Jim Henson said in 1985, as the movie neared completion. "I think we're breaking new ground in a lot of areas, and it's stretching all of our skills a bit farther than we have before. I'm so completely into it right now. But I feel basically puppetry and all the techniques we're using are just opening up doors. There's an enormous wide-open area out there of all kinds of things people can do with this."[7]

Chapter Two

The Long Road to the *Labyrinth* Screenplay

"The writing of the *Labyrinth* script was a strange journey," muses Brian Henson, in what can only be described as an understatement. It may not be a record, but the *Labyrinth* screenplay went through a remarkable number of iterations—estimated at twenty-five—all penned primarily by Jim Henson's friends and colleagues. Although Jim contributed many key story elements, none of the scripts were written by him. "My dad was not particularly good with words," notes Cheryl Henson, one of Henson's three girls. "That's one reason that the scripting was hard. Some of the choices he made were specific to not repeating the 'mistakes' of *Dark Crystal*."

Cheryl says, "That movie was criticized for its script. Originally, the only characters who [did require English subtitles] were the Gelflings, and that didn't work for the audience. After the initial screenings, they had to go back and create and add words for the other characters. So I think this time my father really wanted to work with people who were word masters. To have words that worked. That was important to him."

When writing began, the first person to descend into the labyrinth was Canadian poet Dennis Lee.

ABOVE Concept illustration of the goblin kingdom, rendered by production designer Elliot Scott. **BELOW** Elliot Scott's visualization of Sarah and Hoggle on their journey through the labyrinth. **TOP RIGHT** Elliot Scott's depiction of the labyrinth belies Sarah's initial statement that "it doesn't look that far." **BOTTOM RIGHT** A contentious encounter between Jareth and Hoggle, as conveyed in one of Scott's preproduction illustrations.

From Fraggle to Hoggle

Dennis Lee is a renowned poet and children's author who has won two bronze medals from the Canadian Association of Children's Literature (for the books *Alligator Pie* and *Garbage Delight*), was made an Officer of the Order of Canada, and was Toronto's first poet laureate. His fame as one of the writers of *Labyrinth* has also garnered continued attention over the decades. Lee tends to deflect that attention, humbly noting that the role he played drafting the script was comparatively small. "Jim knew me because of [my work on] *Fraggle Rock*, which was shot in Toronto," he explains. For that groundbreaking TV series, Lee contributed inventive lyrics with zany rhymes. And he was surprised when Henson asked him to fix the script for *The Dark Crystal* during postproduction, rewriting the characters' dialogue.

"For some reason, Jim asked me to take a crack at it," Lee says. "I say 'For some reason' because I had no background in film or TV." To Lee's surprise, his talents jibed nicely with the assignment. "Jim wanted to keep working in this mode of serious fantasy films, as well as Muppet movies," Lee explains. "So he took another wild gamble and invited me to write the script for *Labyrinth*. He had a rough version of the story already in mind, but it was very open-ended. I was involved in early discussions with Jim, Brian Froud, and several others as we explored where the story might go."

In March 1983, Lee, Jim, Brian, and Wendy met to discuss *Labyrinth* at Jim's home in London, where Henson was producing the fourth season of *The Muppet Show*. In this initial meeting, the group conceived of a series of key plot points. A king—initially referred to as "Jen twenty-five years later," a reference to the male Gelfling protagonist in *The Dark Crystal*—is dissatisfied with ruling. The unnamed prince of darkness, a shape-changer (or "shadow-shaper," as Brian Froud puts it), comes to the palace and casts a spell on the king and his jester, Snotweed. Then the dark prince kidnaps the queen—initially referred to as "Kira twenty-five years later," the female Gelfling protagonist in *The Dark Crystal*—and the royal baby (unnamed), and he spirits them away to the Castle of Darkness at the heart of a great labyrinth. "When the king and jester come to, they find themselves in the beginning of a maze," the outline continued. "They make their way ahead, meeting many characters and undergoing many adventures. Meanwhile the queen is growing enamored of her captor, not seeing him for what he is."

ABOVE Elliot Scott's visualization of Taya's—later Sarah's—neighborhood and family home. **OPPOSITE** Elliot Scott's preproduction illustrations depicting Hoggle standing before the Wiseman's chair and a scene where Jareth and his goblins contemplate his new, stripey pajama-wearing acquisition.

Based on this, Lee drafted his first story treatment, which he completed on April 11, 1983. In it, he introduced a world of changes. The central character became Taya, a young girl described as "alive and fifteen and Special"—with a capital S. Lee gave the dark prince a name: Jareth. And Snotweed became Hoggle, "the warty dwarf." Aside from the royal trappings, the story Lee drafted included numerous details that survived the many drafts to come. The vivacious Taya is ordered to become the royal companion to a one-year-old prince. Taya's job as the prince's companion is "to play with him every day, look after his needs, and always to protect him from the wicked wiles of the goblins, who waited everywhere to steal the babies of men—especially a king's baby."

But on the day that Taya is to take her vow as companion, she decides that this is not the way she plans to spend her adolescence. Taya sees no way out of her predicament—the king is adamant—so she goes to the ceremony that will lock her into servitude. But during the ritual, when she is asked if she will protect the child for the space of seven years—or even longer, if called upon—Taya breaks down and refuses. "Ohhh, I wish the goblins would come!" she cries.

This provides Jareth, the king of the goblins (who is disguised as one of the ceremony's priests), with the opening he has long awaited. He steps forward and summons his goblin minions, who spirit the babe away. Horrified, Taya grabs hold of Jareth's cape as he rises into the air, and she is dragged along to his kingdom.

Once there, she loses her grip and falls, landing squarely upon poor Hoggle, the aforementioned dwarf.

Ten days after completing the treatment, Lee submitted a condensed summary of the first six scenes, followed the next day by a memo regarding the story's structure—what he referred to as "foundations." Lee's memo recommended that Taya's character be made a princess, "possibly the king's first daughter." As a result, the king's wife would be Taya's stepmother, and the baby would be her stepbrother.

Six months later, on October 31, 1983, Lee completed his work in the form of a "poetic novella," as Jim Henson referred to it. Lee, however, was less sure of its merits. "I think that glorifies it considerably," he states. "What I passed along to Jim was more atmosphere and verbal evocations than a solid script."

"The truth is," Lee states, "where the challenge of clarifying *Dark Crystal* aligned with my strengths, the challenge of writing a screenplay from scratch aligned with my inexperience and limitations. I simply wasn't the right person for the job, and after a number of months, Jim and I both had the good sense to recognize that. Jim and Brian had powerful hunches about the visual dimension of the film, but that wasn't an area where I could contribute. It soon became clear that being a poet and a lyricist wasn't going to be enough. I patched together what I could, but the next writer had to start with Jim's original story and make his or her way from there."

So a new writer was asked to help, one who possessed a skillset highly attuned to outlandish humor: Monty Python member Terry Jones.

The Python in the Labyrinth

It was a case of great minds thinking alike. Comedian, writer, director, and historian Terry Jones recalled, "I had been thinking about turning my children's book, *Erik the Viking*, into a film, and thought it was something Jim Henson might be interested in. I rang up his office, and they said, 'That's funny—he was trying to reach you yesterday.'"[8]

Henson's daughter Lisa may have had something to do with that. "During that summer I worked with him on script development. He had a few projects, including an idea for a TV show called *Starboppers*. But the big one that he was working on was *Labyrinth*. He was trying to get the story right. He had been working with Dennis Lee and some other *Fraggle Rock* people, and it was not really coming together. It didn't feel like a feature-film screenplay."

Lisa continues, "I felt that it would be nice to make things less of a group-writing situation and put it in the hands of an experienced screenwriter. It might have been my suggestion—or maybe not—but we talked about hiring Terry Jones."

"Jim and I met up," Jones said. "We chatted. Eventually, I agreed to have a go at it." The writing of a new *Labyrinth* screenplay went quickly, according to Jones: "I sat down with Jim's basic storyline and Brian Froud's drawings, and it practically wrote itself. The first draft came out in about three weeks. . . . Whenever I got to a situation where I wanted to invent a character, all I had to do was take Brian's creations and give them words."

This proved to be both a blessing and a curse—at least for the puppeteers in Jim Henson's Creature Shop. Everyone loved Jones's offbeat interpretation of Froud's fantastical characters, but it meant making lots of new puppets. "When we started working on *Labyrinth*, we didn't have the finished script," says Connie Peterson, then production administrator for the Creature Shop, which was already up and running building puppets. "But we knew we needed goblins, so we started making goblins. And then we just kept building everything Jim and Brian thought we'd need."

Brian Froud recalls, "We were close to finishing our puppet build when Terry became inspired by the doodles in my sketchbooks. Well, Jim went with it. And suddenly we were frantically building these doorknockers that spoke and a wild gang of Fireys [flame-colored characters Sarah meets in the labyrinth], and all these other things that were just tiny little doodles in the corners of the sketchbook!"

ABOVE Jim Henson (right) appreciated writer Terry Jones's (left) quirky sense of humor. Assistant director Ken Baker can be seen in the background.

Jones delivered his first script in February 1984. Most of the new characters he added—and their very clever dialogue—wound up on the screen. "Jim really loved Terry's version," says Mira Velimirovic, Jim's creative assistant at the time. "I've got to tell you, it was brilliant—a laugh-out-loud kind of script."

Jones introduced many of the charming creatures that Sarah encounters in the labyrinth: the clumps of lichen that watch her try to find her way; the helpful little worm (who, Jones indicated in the script, has a cockney accent); the little creatures who keep changing the marks that Sarah makes on the bricks of the labyrinth to help find her way; and the playing-card guards Alph and Ralph (and their upside-down counterparts, whom Jones dubbed Alph B and Ralph B; the producers later changed their names to Jim and Tim). And then there's the delightful "Shaft of Hands." Jones's script was fun and highly fanciful. But a few qualities were missing that Jim Henson felt were integral to the story. "Terry and Jim really got on well," says Velimirovic. "But Jim was looking to humanize the script a bit, to bring out the story of the girl."

"We had very different ideas about what we wanted the story to be," Jones said at the time. "Jim wanted it to be about a young girl coming to adolescence and putting her childhood behind her and growing to face the world. That wasn't a story that meant a lot to me."[9]

In Jones's version of the tale, the former Python recalled, "She goes into the labyrinth, and eventually she finds out there is no solution. She keeps thinking she's solved it, and then it keeps cheating on her. The idea in the end is that she finds out there is no solution, you've just got to go with it and enjoy it. And when she gets to the center, she finds out that the character who seemed

all-powerful to begin with isn't all-powerful. In fact, he's someone who uses the labyrinth—which is basically the world—to keep people from getting to his heart. She gets there and annihilates him in the end. So it's about the world, and about people who are more interested in manipulating the world than actually baring themselves at all, having any kind of emotional honesty. Jim didn't get that story at all."[10]

When Jones heard that David Bowie was in line to play Jareth, he realized that his original vision for the Goblin King—a character he hadn't envisioned taking up major screen time—might be greatly modified. Still, Jones recognized that the story wasn't his "baby" to begin with. He also fully acknowledged that the visual interpretation of his ideas surpassed all of his expectations. "In a way, my best contribution was just starting off something that the puppet-makers made much better and improved. I just started the ball rolling."[11]

LEFT Work on the main puppet characters began long before *Labyrinth*'s script was finalized. A rough size comparison chart illustrated by Sherry Amott (which included the film's as-yet uncast human female protagonist) was provided to help the fabricators work up prototypes for Ludo, Didymus, and Hoggle. **ABOVE** An unused concept sketch by Scott depicts Sarah relaxing in a candlelit boudoir. **BELOW** Scott's concept for the underground cavern that's lined with the stone faces known as False Alarms.

Getting to the Heart of the Matter

Though Jones's script was lively, it didn't provide much insight into Sarah, the central character. As Henson began tweaking Jones's drafts, he also invited Laura Phillips, a *Fraggle Rock* writer with a knack for relationship-driven stories, to try her hand at a rewrite. By August 1984, she completed her first draft.

Phillips fleshed out the heroine's missing inner life and her interests outside the labyrinth. For the most part, both Lee and Jones had defined her solely by her heroic task—looking after the baby. Phillips provided insight into what a teenage girl would rather be doing besides babysitting, and her draft came closer to

evoking the emotional journey that Henson wanted to portray on screen. However, Phillips didn't get all the way there, and Henson continued to invite feedback, soliciting notes and ideas from, among others, fellow puppeteer Frank Oz, Bernie Brillstein, Brian and Wendy Froud, Lisa Henson, Lawrence Mirkin (producer of *Fraggle Rock* and *The Jim Henson Hour*), and Mira Velimirovic. Henson also asked his executive producer George Lucas for input.

ABOVE Brian Froud's early concept painting hints that the character of Sarah is playful and quite comfortable around monsters and goblins.

"It was one of those days when you try to take everything apart and put it back together again," recalls Velimirovic of the conversation at one of those meetings. "Everyone at that time was really taken with [American mythologist] Joseph Campbell, particularly George. And he looked at the film as a kind of archetypal story, a young girl coming to terms with being female."

"I liked the coming-of-age aspect of Sarah's story," George Lucas says today. "It's a classic story. It's not quite a classic archetype, but it is definitely part of the rites of motherhood and other fairy-tale stories about girls."

"George came in when we were still struggling with the script," Jim Henson said during postproduction on the film. "Terry Jones did several drafts, then Laura Phillips, and about that time George came in and worked a good deal on the script."[12]

With all these cooks seasoning the broth, it was sometimes difficult to tell if the tweaks were making the story better or worse. For example, although Laura Phillips's efforts strengthened the screenplay's structure, they unraveled some of Jones's witty dialogue. As a result, Terry Jones was called in to have another go at the script.

He addressed Jim's comments and at the same time removed some of Phillips's emotional beats in favor of reinserting his funny bits. Phillips, in turn, revised Jones's revision. In a memo that Larry Mirkin later sent to the Henson archives, he recalls that at one crucial point, Phillips suggested cutting the Escher room scene. Jim's response, Mirkin notes, was, "for Jim, apoplectic. He said words to the effect that 'if you think we should cut that scene, you don't understand this film.' It was just a conversation, but Laura got the message."

Eventually, Jim realized that an objective—and accomplished—voice was required. "So Elaine came in," says Brian Henson.

ABOVE The exterior wall of the labyrinth, near the pond where Sarah meets Hoggle, as rendered by Scott. **OPPOSITE** Title page for the film's shooting script, which notes "Cuts and first revision by E.M." (Elaine May).

The Literary Fairy Godmother

Elaine May is a renowned comedian, writer, and director who was once part of a groundbreaking comedic duo with Mike Nichols. At the time, she was also a script doctor of the highest caliber, known for her contributions to such lauded scripts as *Heaven Can Wait*, *Reds*, and *Tootsie*. "She flew in in the dark of night and stayed in our house and worked in an upper room," Brian Henson says. "She worked with my father for two or three days, flat out, to try to bring back the comedy but retain the better structure. All of this happened when we were really close to shooting."

"It was very late in the process," confirms Velimirovic. "Elaine did a quick—and I mean shockingly quick—rewrite that was very subtle. But the touches that she added were very humanizing. It somehow made Sarah a more authentic girl, and I think that Jim felt greatly relieved."

The final script—which incorporated May's comments and many others—was dated April 11, 1985. Principal photography began a few days later at London's Elstree Studios on April 15.

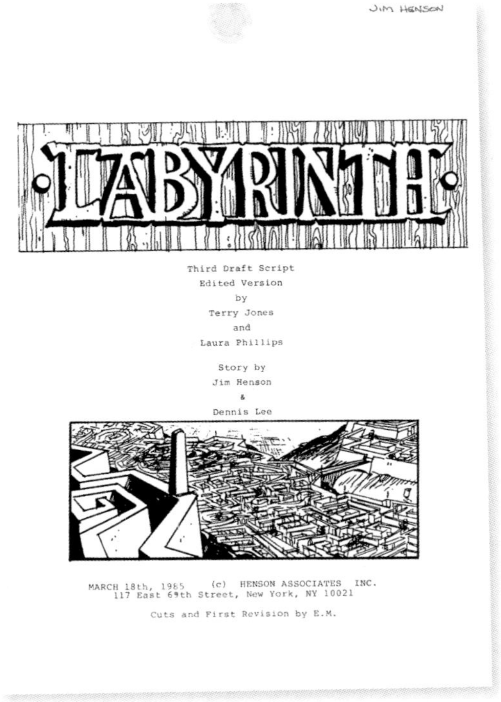
JIM HENSON

LABYRINTH

Third Draft Script
Edited Version
by
Terry Jones
and
Laura Phillips

Story by
Jim Henson
&
Dennis Lee

MARCH 18th, 1985 (c) HENSON ASSOCIATES INC.
117 East 69th Street, New York, NY 10021

Cuts and First Revision by E.M.

Chapter Three

Jim Henson's Creature Shop

Fabrication of the puppets that populate the world of *Labyrinth* was ongoing throughout the scripting process. Dozens of puppets were built from scratch, along with almost every item in the Goblin King's realm, from rocks to trees to weapons to wardrobe. The fabrication occurred at a facility across from Jim Henson's London home, the origins of which predated *Labyrinth* by several years.

In 1979, *The Muppet Show* was shooting in London, so Jim had moved to the city, making his home in Hampstead, a well-to-do village. Fortuitously, he came across the perfect location for his new workshop—a former postal-sorting facility right across the street from his house. After extensive restructuring of the building's large interior, a crew of artists moved in to begin designing Skeksis and Gelflings for *The Dark Crystal*.

It didn't take long for the puppet builders to enter into a whole new area of creative invention. "The characters are just not Muppets at all," Henson noted at the time. "We hesitate to call them puppets even. . . . Instead, we're trying to go toward a sense of realism—toward a reality of creatures that are actually alive, and we're mixing up puppetry and all kinds of other techniques [to create] something that people will actually believe."[13]

The question arose: What should these unprecedented creations be called?

Henson decided, for the moment, to call them creatures. The name stuck; it fit the work—and the workshop, too, which soon became known as Jim Henson's Creature Shop.

ABOVE AND FOLLOWING SPREAD An assortment of goblin puppets, each labeled with an identification tag, assembled in the Creature Shop. **RIGHT** Costumer and fabricator Val Jones grooms the Wiseman's impressive eyebrows.

FUR

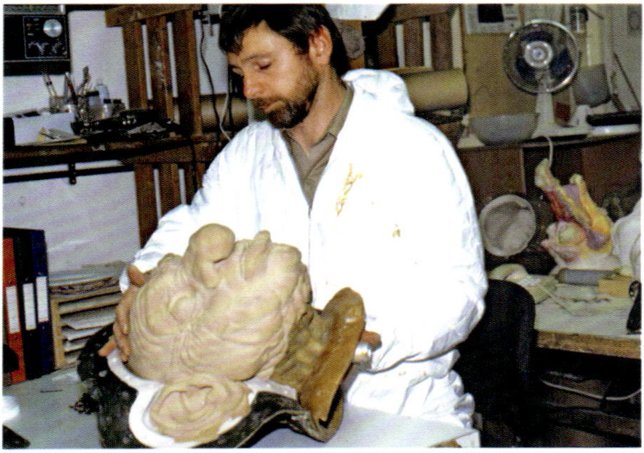

In July 1983, the *Labyrinth* crew consisted of five people: four veterans of *The Dark Crystal*—Brian and Wendy Froud, Sherry Amott, and Michael McCormick—as well as Connie Peterson, the new production administrator. "I was the stranger in the mix," Peterson says. Soon, Faz Fazakas, the New York shop's resident electromechanical genius who'd pioneered their animatronic puppet-control systems, flew over to help them get started. He spent weeks measuring floor thicknesses to determine the best locations for all the heavy equipment.

"We had an area with band saws, belt sanders, and bench grinders," Peterson recalls. "And we had a room for making fiberglass. We had an entire machine shop devoted to metals, a sewing machine room, and a knitting machine room. And our foam and plaster shop was in the basement."

But it wasn't all work, work, work. "Once we set up the workshop, we played. I mean, we played," says designer Brian Froud. "That was coming from the tradition of Muppets. What I mean by play is, we'd put a couple of bits of Ping-Pong ball on a stick and wiggle it around. Suddenly it's a creature. It's alive. So we were always thinking about, 'Well, what sort of creatures could we make?' And then it's, 'Well, we could use an eyeball on something.' And then someone will say, "Whoa, what if we have lots of eyeballs!' And you go, 'Great!' And then you think, 'Oh. Right. Now we've gotta make 'em!' What was great about it was, we all had fun making stuff. Because we were playing."

LEFT (top to bottom) Ludo's foam face takes shape under the skilled hands of fabricator Stuart Robinson. Foam mold designer Michael Osborn removes a Hoggle mask from its plaster mold. Senior puppet builder Jane Gootnick checks the detailing on Didymus's wardrobe. **RIGHT** Puppet designer Ross Hill "plants" the many-eyed lichen creature that he built, inspired by Brian Froud's design. **FOLLOWING SPREAD** Jim Henson's Creature Shop operates like a factory in full production mode.

FRAGILE

Chapter Four

Characters & Creatures

bug pattern + jewels
bone shirt
armour
sling cape
blue leather
gauntlet
tan boots
waistcoat
loose
tight
1983
LABYRINTH
GOBLIN KING
DAVID BOWIE
Jareth
Brian Froud

EARLY JARETH IDEA.

Jareth

"Just fear me, love me, do as I say—and I will be your slave." – JARETH

PERFORMER: DAVID BOWIE

The candidates for the role of *Labyrinth*'s Goblin King read like a who's who of top concert draws from the early 1980s: Michael Jackson, Sting, David Bowie, David Lee Roth, Rod Stewart, Mick Jagger, Roger Daltrey, Freddie Mercury, Prince, and Ted Nugent. All famous, all rock 'n' roll stars, all perfect for a large amphitheater. How did their names end up on a list of individuals to play the Goblin King? The answer goes back to a discussion that Jim had with *Labyrinth* composer Trevor Jones.

"At one point," Jones recalls, "I mentioned to [Jim] that having completed a major symphonic orchestral score for *Dark Crystal*, I was keen to work on a rock score." Henson listened with interest to Jones's idea about a musically contemporary approach to fantasy. "We discussed the idea of a central rock artist who was also an actor on-screen along with puppets," says Jones, "and several names came up—among them Mick Jagger and David Bowie."

The idea of using a rock star clearly resonated with Jim. Brian Henson recalls his father canvassing him and others for opinions. "I remember that I told my dad that David Bowie was the most interesting possibility," Brian says. "I think my dad was really

LEFT Early concepts by Brian Froud for the Goblin King ranged from fantastical beasts to dark and brooding wizards in horned headgear. Froud also served served as one of the film's costume designers, as indicated in these sketches of Jareth's dashing Byronic wardrobe. Jareth's look would be greatly modified once David Bowie was cast in the role. **ABOVE** Watching a playback is always serious business.

impressed at how courageous David was. The biggest concern that you have when you cast a music artist in an acting role is whether or not they are scared of being completely vulnerable. The greatest actors are the ones who are not. And it was clear that David was completely comfortable onstage." Bowie continued to communicate with Henson throughout the lengthy scripting process, but he held off actually signing on to the role until he saw a close-to-final script. Finally, the deal was set on February 15, with filming just two months away.

Bowie was quite pleased with the character of Jareth as depicted in the screenplay. "Jareth is the Goblin King," Bowie explained in 1986. "One feels that he's rather reluctantly inherited the position of being Goblin King, as though he would really rather be—I don't know—down in Soho or something. But he's not. His thing in life is to be the Goblin King, and he runs the whole place as well as he can. . . . He gets everything his own way."[14]

"David's performance as Jareth is powerful," Jim said during filming. "His role is similar to being the leader of a gang. Everyone in the kingdom does what he says until Sarah comes along—and she defies him. The goblins David controls are like members of his gang. He treats them terribly, but they do anything he says."[15]

Brian Froud's first meeting with Bowie convinced him that they'd chosen the right man to play the Goblin King. "It was in his dressing room," recalls Froud. "The workshop had made him a little flute out of bone, and I gave it to him. His immediate response was delight, and he leaped up onto the dressing table, crouched down, and played some notes. Behind him, I remember, he was framed by the lightbulbs that go around the mirror. The dressing room was a prosaic place, but suddenly there was magic in the room! It was an astonishing transformation.

"Before me hunkered an evocation of Pan! My heart leaped and my instinct was to step back. Then David laughed his 'Bowie' laugh and climbed back down. The spell was broken and he was just David again—but I had momentarily been transported to an ancient mythological space, where fauns and satyrs were tangible. Our Goblin King was no longer a figment of our creative imaginings. And I thought, 'Oh! We're going to be all right now.'"

Brian and fellow designer Ellis Flyte helped define Jareth's look. "The Goblin King has a unique and very unusual style," Flyte says. "We demonstrated that with jewelry, rather than a crown—an ear piece, a wrist piece, an ornate brooch, and so on. And we created

RIGHT TOP The script, David Bowie explained, attracted him to the role. "I found it very amusing," he said during filming. "It's by Terry Jones, of Monty Python, and it has that kind of slightly inane insanity running through it."

RIGHT BOTTOM Sometimes he cried and sometimes he didn't. Young Toby Froud's emotions ran the gamut, even in the arms of David Bowie.

something that looked vaguely spinal at the back of his neck. It appeared to be an integral part of his body, with an organic quality."

Brian created possibly the most defining element of Jareth's wardrobe. "I was scheduled to be onstage somewhere recently," Brian says. "And when I came out, there was applause. I said, 'Yes, I am that man who designed the pants for David Bowie!' Everybody cheered." Jareth's pants are undeniably tight, undeniably revealing, and at first glance, almost over the line for an adult male character in a film with a teenage heroine. "We got in a bit of trouble about how tight his pants were," Brian admits, "but the choice was deliberate."

Within the context of the film, Brian explains, those pants represent Sarah's innocent imagination. "We're not looking at reality. We're inside this girl's head. Jareth has the tight pants because he is many, many things that a teenaged girl relates to. He is a rock star, and he is also a leather jacket guy—a classic 'bad boy'—and he's Heathcliff, and also a ballet dancer. I gave him a swagger stick that has a crystal ball on it, but if you look at it closely, it's a microphone! There are a lot of subtleties going on in there, but it was always this romantic figure that I was after. He was never quite real. He's an amalgam of the inner fantasies of this girl."

"He's the bad boy," adds Brian Henson. "You can't help but be attracted to the bad boy. But it's scary for Sarah. That's the important part about it. That's what my dad was trying to do there."

"There's a point in the movie," says Brian Froud, "where the relationship changes. We sort of get that when we arrive at the ballroom scene. Because once Jareth becomes sexual, he's dangerous.... That's what gives this power to his character. It's interesting how over the years people constantly respond to it. It speaks to generations and generations of young girls. It's precisely the thing that we had been a bit nervous about portraying. But it really works."

ABOVE Despite Bowie's being, at the time, one of the world's biggest music stars, his coworkers always found him approachable. "And it was wonderful watching him shoot, varying his performance from take to take," Jennifer Connelly said in 1985.

Sarah

"Oh, it's not fair!"—SARAH

PERFORMER: JENNIFER CONNELLY

Jim Henson saw many, many actresses audition for the role of Sarah. Auditions ran from April 1984 to January 1985, in both the UK and the United States. Many of the young actresses within this amazingly talented group would become household names within just a few years, including Helena Bonham Carter, Mary Stuart Masterson, Sarah Jessica Parker, Laura San Giacomo, Laura Dern, Marisa Tomei, Jane Krakowski, Yasmine Bleeth, Ally Sheedy, and Mia Sara.

"During a lot of the casting sessions, we had the actresses perform a scene between Sarah and Didymus, because we already had a Didymus puppet in a prototype phase," recalls Brian Henson.

However, Jim Henson couldn't quite envision any of these women as Sarah. Then Jennifer Connelly came in to read in January 1985 and hit a home run. Henson cast her within a week.

"When you're casting a part like Sarah . . . you hope someone walks in the door and is the right person," Jim Henson enthused. "And when Jenny walked in, she was the right person, and it was one of those great little moments. She did a wonderful reading, and she's a bright, intelligent actress who takes direction well, and everything was just right. . . . I found I could talk very straight to her. We could talk about her performance. I didn't have to tiptoe around her feelings or anything like that. She could talk, you know, just as an adult."[16]

BELOW Conceptual designer Brian Froud's early impressions of goblin architectural details, and behind the door, two of the film's main protagonists.

"It was a very hard role to fully understand," notes executive producer George Lucas, "in that there are a lot of things that are buried in the character, but aren't ever expressed. And for a young actress to get that is very difficult. And yet Jennifer was very good at that."[17]

"Jennifer was absolutely right for the part of Sarah," observed David Bowie. "She's a really good actress. And she's a pleasure to work with. And it's a big strain, a film like this. And every day, without fail, she was on form. I mean, she's absolutely terrific."

Connelly recalls enjoying the filming experience. "The whole thing was kind of like a wonderland for me because I was at the perfect age for it," she says. "All the jumping, climbing, running around, falling down the shaft, wearing the harnesses, and flying around on wires—I loved all of it!"

ABOVE The play that Sarah is rehearsing at the beginning of the film is called *The Labyrinth*, which lends credence to Jim Henson's suggestion that her adventures in the maze may have been a dream, inspired by her recent activities. **RIGHT** Beauty and the beast: Connelly and Ludo.

She continues, "And Jim always had time to explain things, which is something I found remarkable. It was a very gentle process, very collaborative. I didn't really expect it to be that way." During the production, Connelly felt that Henson really "got" her. "I think he understood me very well," she commented during a 1986 interview. "Maybe because he has a daughter exactly my age. His daughter and I are only one week apart in age. He was very good at catching what I was feeling."[18]

"I think that part of it was a bit of a valentine to his kids, especially his daughters," explains Mira Velimirovic, Henson's creative assistant. "He wanted to do a magical world that was the creation of and the creation for a young girl who's at that particular age . . . fourteen, fifteen, part girl, part young woman."[19]

Many of the film's fans, particularly the female fans, identify with Sarah, warts and all. "Sarah is, in fact, very flawed," Cheryl Henson says. "But I think that's part of why they like her. My father was speaking from his heart. He was living with three young women when he was working on the film, and that probably made a difference in the level of honesty in the depiction. I think it's significant that he had three daughters who went through that same period of their lives that Sarah is going through. My mother used to say that *Labyrinth* is the most personal of all my father's films."

Although reflections of each of his children pop up in the film, *Labyrinth* is, and was intended to be, the tale of a young girl finding her way through the center of a fantasy. That, in itself, made the film something of a rarity. Whereas many classic fairy tales and literary fantasies focus on female protagonists, cinematic fantasies usually focus on boys, reflecting, possibly, a corporate studio belief that films about male protagonists sell more tickets.

As Jim Henson observed, "The movie is about a person at the point of changing from being a child to a woman. I think that's a pretty magic time, right at that point. Times of transition are always magic. Twilight is a magic time. Dawn is magic. It's that time between sleeping and dreaming. There are mystical qualities related to that. And the film is about going through that little period of transition. You can't really have a person grow up and mature over the course of an evening, or an hour-and-a-half movie, but it's about one little element of maturing—and in Sarah's case, taking responsibility for her life."[20]

RIGHT (top to bottom) Jennifer Connelly's enthusiasm never flagged while she was on set. The actress and the director experienced a comfortable rapport throughout filming. Jim Henson and Jennifer Connelly on the Escher set, distinguishable by the low-relief sculpture on the doorway in the background. Though the initial writers made Sarah something of a beleaguered fairy-tale princess, Laura Phillips managed to transform her into a modern teenager. "Everyone on the crew, from all the different sectors—special effects, puppetry, camera— was so open to me," said Connelly in 1985. "They were all ready and willing to teach me."

Toby

"He's a lively little chap. I think I'll call him Jareth. He's got my eyes."—JARETH

PERFORMER: TOBY FROUD
VOICE: TOBY FROUD (CRYING), DAVID BOWIE (GURGLING)

Being regularly approached by strangers who wish to ask about an important event in your past—one that you can't remember—can be disconcerting. This has been Toby Froud's fate, though there are far worse things than having played the baby in *Labyrinth*.

"I don't think that I have any mental scars from it," Toby comments good-naturedly. "I don't have any phobias of staircases or crystal balls. I can remember seeing goblins' faces and chaos all around, but that could be from seeing the film so many times. I've always known that the baby was me. I watched the film from the time I was three or four years old, and I remember being told it was me. I remember there were props from the film in our house—three-dimensional sculptures and paintings of the creatures from *Labyrinth* and *Dark Crystal*. They were all very familiar to me."

You might say, despite escaping from Jareth's clutches, Toby wound up being raised by goblins and fairies after all. In a way, that was almost preordained. His parents, Brian and Wendy Froud, fell in love and got married during preproduction of *The Dark Crystal*. Then, in 1982, after brainstorming with Jim Henson about the likely premise of Henson's next fantasy film, Brian went home and drew an illustration of a lovely little baby surrounded by goblins. Flash forward to 1984, and during preproduction on *Labyrinth*, the Frouds gave birth to a lovely little baby boy—who happened to look a great deal like the baby in the painting.

TOP LEFT The once and future babe: The child in Brian Froud's first artistic rendering for Labyrinth bore an uncanny resemblance to his yet-to-be-conceived son, eventually cast as baby Toby. **BOTTOM LEFT** Even when surrounded by fantastical creatures, Toby stands out thanks to his distinctive costume. **ABOVE** Henson wields a balloon in hopes of eliciting a giggle from his young method actor Toby, with mom, Wendy Froud, watching.

Flash forward another year, and Brian says, "We'd been working away, and Toby was about a year old. We'd spent maybe three years developing and building things and raising money for *Labyrinth*. Suddenly, we were ready to start filming, and we realized we needed a baby. And I said, 'Well, look—I have one in the cupboard!'"

Brian continues, "It was weird that Toby was exactly the age we'd always envisioned the baby in the story. He was also very comfortable around puppets and the strangeness of being on a film set. So Jim said, 'Oh—we should use him!'"

Toby received the royal treatment on the set. Wendy, his mom, always stayed close by, and he had several additional "wranglers" keeping an eye on him. "That's one thing that we hadn't anticipated," Brian says. "We wanted a baby who would crawl, but by the time we started shooting, Toby suddenly started to walk, and he had to be wrangled and corralled."

The young actor also had his own stand-in—the baby of puppet builder Amy Van Gilder—and he had a "stunt double"—a doll made by Wendy—for the scene where Jareth carelessly tosses Sarah's little brother into the air.

ABOVE Bowie teaches Toby a tricky dance move. **RIGHT** Wendy Froud was always on hand to wrangle her baby son on the set.

Toby also had a custom-made wardrobe, designed by his father to serve a very specific purpose. "The baby needed to be wearing something that would stand out among all the goblins and strange shapes," Brian Froud explains. "Something that would say, 'That's the baby,' when he was way out in the distance. So I designed the red-and-white stripy outfit."

Brian continues, "There were baby 'jammies' that you could buy, but we needed several exact duplicates, and none of the stripes matched up on the purchased ones. They were always different. So we bought material and made absolute duplicate costumes. Well, when we put it on Toby, we realized that the usual diapers were just too bulky underneath, which looked ridiculous. So then we cobbled together a slimmed-down diaper. Everything looked great."

Brian still laughs over what happened next. "Of course, on the first day of shooting, David Bowie was standing near Wendy, and she was holding Toby. And the first thing that Toby did was pee all over David. That was his introduction to David, because the diaper was useless. It was too thin. It was the beginning of their relationship." Today, Toby laughs, too, and says, "I get asked the question, and I just say, 'Yes, I peed on David Bowie.'"

For some people, having your parents tell stories about you—in front of crowds at puppetry conventions, fairy conventions, Comic-Con, and so forth—might be embarrassing, but not for Toby, who says he got used to it early on. These days, as one of cinema's most-famous babies, he tells the same stories about himself when he gives talks about his own career as a sculptor, fabricator, puppeteer, and filmmaker. Toby also founded his own production company, named Stripey Pajama Productions. "I couldn't resist naming it that," he confesses. "Actually, I really don't think I had a choice."

Hoggle

"I ain't never been no one's friend before."—HOGGLE

PUPPETEERS: SHARI WEISER, BRIAN HENSON, ROBERT TYGNER, DAVID GREENAWAY, AND MAK WILSON

VOICE: BRIAN HENSON

CREATURE SHOP TEAM: TONY DUNSTERVILLE, VALERIE CHARLTON, TADEUSZ KRZANOWSKI, POLLY SMITH, MARION APPLETON, TOM NEWBY, DEBORAH HARKNESS

"Hoggle," *Labyrinth*'s production notes state, "is a dwarf to remember. He is less than four feet small, old, ugly, cantankerous, selfish, infuriating, childish, and cowardly. But he can also be, when the situation demands, shrewd, clever, quite brave, loyal, nice, and with a heart of gold." He was also, according to Jim Henson at the time, "the most complicated puppet creature we've ever built."[21]

That "puppet creature" consisted of two very different and separate parts: the head and the body. The head was operated from off camera via radio control; twenty-two-year-old Shari Weiser was the performer who operated the body from inside it. "Hoggle's body fit me like a pregnancy pad on steroids," the three-foot-two-inch-tall actress says today.

"His hands always were a problem," Jim Henson explained during production, "because Shari has very small hands. So we built these sort of large hands over hers. But because Hoggle was the most complicated character, we were trying to do more with him. He had to be virtually the second lead in the film."

Tom Newby—who was part of the electromechanical team at the New York Muppet Workshop, which was later renamed Jim Henson's Creature Shop in New York—flew to England to create mechanical gloves for Hoggle. These long, skeleton-like metal armatures fit over Weiser's hands, so that when she bent her wrists back, the hand opened, and when she bent her wrists forward, the hand closed. "The gloves were a nightmare," Weiser says. "They were very clumsy. They worked on little gears, so when I moved my fingers, the outer fingers curled. It was like having those closet reachers attached to your hands."

LEFT Hoggle's practice of spraying fairies as if they were pesky insects initially gives Sarah a negative impression of him. **ABOVE** Shari Weiser, sans Hoggle head.

One scene—where Hoggle catches a poisoned peach—proved to be the most difficult of all. However, that was because of the growing camaraderie between Brian Henson, the puppeteer doing Hoggle's voice, and the film's resident rock star, David Bowie. "When Jareth throws the peach to Hoggle and Hoggle catches it," Brian Henson explains, "Hoggle is supposed to say, 'What is it?' And then Jareth replies, 'It's a peach.' Well, for whatever reason, the idea that you're looking at a peach, and you still say, 'What is it?' began to feel absurd to both David and me. I mean, it's a peach, is what it is. And for whatever reason, that really struck us as funny. We kept cracking up."

Brian wasn't originally assigned to voice Hoggle, but he stepped in when the first actor proved too difficult to work with, because he kept improvising dialogue during rehearsals. Because Brian was already operating Hoggle's mouth, it seemed natural for him to say Hoggle's lines. "Shari was inside the costume, and she did all the body movement," Brian says, "but even though her head was in Hoggle's head, her jaw wasn't connected to his jaw. . . . The creature's face was actually radio-controlled by four other members of the crew. Hoggle was the first fully wireless character that we made," Brian explains.

In addition to operating the character's mouth, Brian Henson also was responsible for certain facial expressions. He wore an electronic mitt on his right hand, which he squeezed to work Hoggle's jaw. The mitt acted as a lever; when he pushed it forward, the mouth smiled, and when he pulled it back, the mouth made

ABOVE (left to right) Puppeteer Brian Henson, who uses radio control to puppeteer Hoggle's facial expressions from a distance, moves in closer to confer with Shari Weiser. With their amused director looking on, Jareth and Hoggle have a nose-to-nose confrontation. **RIGHT** Hoggle's practice of spraying fairies as if they were pesky insects initially gives Sarah a negative impression of him.

the dwarf look sad or cross. To create other expressions, team members Robert Tygner, David Greenaway, and Mak Wilson each controlled specific parts of Hoggle's mouth, eyes, and nose. "Everyone involved with designing, building, and especially operating Hoggle had to have the same personality response in mind," Brian Henson says.

Meanwhile, the woman with her head in Hoggle's head had further problems. "I had no peripheral vision at all," Shari says. "And I couldn't look down or up. I could just see straight ahead. So they tried a bunch of different ways to make it easier for me to see."

"We took two eyepieces from a video camera, and we hooked them up inside the head, so Shari would have one against each eye," Brian Henson recalls. "Then we put a video camera inside Hoggle's stomach, pointing straight forward, so she could see what Hoggle would have been seeing. But the visual didn't change when she turned her head—it only changed if she turned her whole body. . . . Finally, we took out the mouth interior pieces and put black makeup on her face. That way she could see out of the mouth whenever it was open."

Brian says, "I've had people approach me and say, 'How did you come up with the way Hoggle talks? He's always grunting and moaning and yowling.' And I say, 'That's the only way Shari could see! We had to keep finding excuses for him to open his mouth, so that Shari could watch where she was going. Hoggle literally had to keep grunting.'"

Didymus

SCHWIK!

Sir Didymus and Ambrosius

"Fear not, fair maiden! I will save thee!"—SIR DIDYMUS

"Ambrosius! Come here right now! You're embarrassing me!"—SIR DIDYMUS

SIR DIDYMUS PUPPETEERS: DAVE GOELZ, DAVID BARCLAY, KAREN PRELL, AND MICHAEL QUINN

VOICE: DAVID SHAUGHNESSY

CREATURE SHOP TEAM: JANE GOOTNICK, DAVID BARCLAY, MARIAN KEATING, NEAL SCANLAN, POLLY SMITH, MARION APPLETON, JUNE KIRBY

AMBROSIUS PUPPETEERS: STEVE WHITMIRE, KEVIN CLASH

VOICE: PERCY EDWARDS
CREATURE SHOP TEAM: MARIAN KEATING

Sir Didymus is the guardian of the bridge that traverses the Bog of Eternal Stench. At first glance, he appears to be a dog. Or perhaps a fox. Or even a squirrel.

Didymus's indeterminate species can be attributed to Brian Froud, who painted a glorious squirrel-ish likeness of the character in 1983. However, Didymus took on additional attributes while being fabricated in the Creature Shop: a lush coat of auburn fur and a pointy nose reminiscent of a red fox's. And the longer puppet designer Jane Gootnick worked on the gallant little beast, the more he reminded her of a feisty canine. After Gootnick consulted with Froud, the foxy squirrel became more of a fox terrier, able to bare his teeth, snarl, and yap with the best of them.

TOP LEFT The likeness of noble Sir Didymus is slowly formed in the pages of Brian Froud's sketchbook. **BOTTOM LEFT** Working from Brian Froud's sketches of Didymus, artist John Stevenson drew these "model sheets" that showed how Didymus might look in action. **ABOVE** A compelling Brian Froud painting of Didymus holding off a much larger goblin foe with his trusty staff.

Didymus was one of the first puppets the shop created during *Labyrinth*'s eighteen months of preproduction. He is recklessly fierce toward his foes—but loyal and gallant to his friends. He's also something of a dandy, clothed in a dashing blue velvet hat with a yellow feather plume, a scarlet doublet with black-and-gold chevrons on the sleeves and epaulets on his shoulders, black gauntlet gloves, and knee armor. "His wardrobe was created by Polly Smith," explains Connie Peterson. "Polly's a fabulous designer, with a wonderful sense of color and style and fabric choice. She made that wonderful blanket and saddle on Didymus's canine steed Ambrosius as well."

Described in the shooting script as "Sir Didymus's trusty steed," the shaggy sheepdog Ambrosius is "fleet and sure-footed in battle, loyal and obedient (except when he sees a cat)." Two flesh-and-blood Old English sheepdogs appear in *Labyrinth*; the dogs took turns playing both Sarah's dog, Merlin, and Ambrosius. One was a beautiful pedigreed pooch provided by a dog-rental company; the other was a near twin. A third sheepdog also appears: a beautiful life-sized puppet built by Marian Keating. The puppet was used for sequences requiring specific feats of thespian skill that were a bit out of range for a real dog. Keating covered the Ambrosius puppet primarily with the silky hair of Icelandic sheep, whereas bits of fake fur enhanced those areas where the dog's coat was a bit shorter.

The Ambrosius puppet's head—which could be operated independently for shots where the nervous animal was peeking around a corner—was made of patterned foam. "There wasn't a sculpted head under all that hair," says Connie Peterson. "We made it from a flat pattern, which is how we make a whole lot of our puppets that don't have to involve foam latex. It's sheet foam that is cut and put together, just like you'd put together clothes."

"We made a saddle to fit the real dog," Peterson says, "because there are scenes where he is walking through the set with Didymus riding on him. And to keep Didymus upright—and not sliding off to the side—we had to make a girdle to go over the sheepdog and under the saddle in order to mush all that fur down. That's how we made sure the puppet had a really firm purchase on the dog."

LEFT (left to right) A study in canine contrast: courageous Sir Didymus and cowardly Ambrosius, each lovable in his own way. **RIGHT** Brian Froud's colorful sketch of Ambrosius.

"Shooting the scenes where Didymus is riding the puppet version of Ambrosius was very much like shooting some of those old Western movies," says Steve Whitmire, one of the two puppeteers who performed as Ambrosius. "The shots were designed to frame the rider rather than what he was riding on. Occasionally, Ambrosius would lift his head up into the frame if he was supposed to do something, or look at something, but mostly he served as a vehicle in those shots—a seat for Didymus."

To make a puppet seem "real," a puppeteer often gives their character human characteristics that people can identify with. For Ambrosius, *Labyrinth* involved intercutting between shots of a dog puppet and a real dog, which made for tricky transitions. Whitmire explains, "If you anthropomorphize your character's performance too much, it won't match the shots with the real dog."

Puppeteer Kevin Clash also performed Ambrosius, and he worked in a semiprone position, close to the ground, most of the time. That year, London was particularly cold, and Clash insists that it actually snowed in August. "The weather was bad," he says. "I remember laying on my side on this rolling cart. Dave Goelz, who operated Didymus, was working beside me, sitting up with his hand going through Ambrosius, so it looked like Didymus was sitting on the dog's back. But . . . I was so low to the ground, and the ground was so cold that I was getting sick constantly. I've never gotten so many colds in my life!"

PREVIOUS SPREAD Veteran puppeteer Dave Goelz (right) was the primary puppeteer for Didymus; for several scenes, Karen Prell (left) assisted Goelz by operating the heroic pup's right paw. **ABOVE** A member of the crew wrangles the flesh-and-blood canine that plays Ambrosius. **RIGHT** Working with two puppets in very close proximity is business as usual for puppeteers Kevin Clash (Ambrosius) and Dave Goelz (Didymus).

Longtime Henson puppeteer Dave Goelz operated at least five puppets during the production, including Didymus. "I played him the way he seemed to be written. He's officious, but not all that cognizant of the big picture. That's what I had fun with—the sense that the other characters could throw him a curve ball and he wouldn't quite know what to do."

In the end, the workshop created three different types of Didymus puppets: a hand puppet with a cast foam-latex head, with cable controls for facial expressions; a radio-controlled armature puppet that could be posed on the real dog playing Ambrosius; and a marionette worked by strings from above by David Barclay, assisted by Ian Thom. The marionette stepped in for shots showing the entire character. Goelz spent most of his time working with the Didymus hand puppet; one hand-controlled the rod that operated his left arm, while his other hand-worked the mouth, the mustache, and movements of the snout. He was assisted by Karen Prell, who operated Didymus's right arm; David Barclay, on the radio-controlled eyebrows; and Michael Quinn, who controlled the eye that wasn't covered by the character's rakish black eye patch. Goelz also radio-controlled the armature's head turns and mouth movements.

"We always used a cable crew of at least three people on a puppet—maybe four, if you needed someone to operate the ears," Goelz says. "Each feature of a creature would be activated by one person working one push-pull cable. Pushing it one way would create a sneer, for example, and pushing it the other way would return it to normal. At the same time, somebody else would be using another cable to make the eyes move, and another person was doing the blinks."

Coordinating a creature's expressions wasn't easy. Goelz says, "Before *Dark Crystal*, we hadn't done characters that had to be performed by so many people. To develop the performances, we had to rehearse the material one line at a time, and plan beats within the dialogue. So perhaps we would decide that as the puppet says the third word, that's when the sneer happens. And then there'd be a beat where the eyes blink twice and then he looks to the right—then looks forward again and speaks. It takes a lot of rehearsal.

"We worked on Didymus for at least a week, maybe two. During the course of rehearsal, the group congeals, and you get to the point where you can pretty much ad-lib. You all feel the others' rhythms. Over time, it all becomes second nature. It's amazing—really something to witness."

LEFT Jim Henson supervises as the radio-controlled armature of Didymus rides the real-life dog playing Ambrosius.

Ludo

"Rocks . . . friends!"—LUDO

PUPPETEERS: RON MUECK, ROB MILLS

VOICE: RON MUECK

CREATURE SHOP TEAM: TIM WHEELER, MICHAEL OSBORN, STUART ROBINSON, VAL JONES, CAS WILLING, LESJA LIBER, JIM SANDYS, MICHAEL WARD, VICKY STOCKWELL, MARION APPLETON

With his big, furry body, which looks like a cross between a grizzly bear and a gorilla, the character of Ludo can seem extremely fierce, but at heart, he's really just "a big lovable lug with a highly expressive mug," as his puppet fabricators refer to him.[22] His expressive face conveys a range of emotions, from sweet goofiness to utter bewilderment.

Ludo stands over eight feet tall when erect—and even then, the knuckles of his gigantic hands still drag on the ground, making him, according to Jim Henson, "one of the biggest things we've ever made for a single person to operate." Henson continued: "The final weight [was] well over seventy-five pounds. Rob Mills and Ron Mueck are just about the same size and shape physically, so they were able to trade off in the part. As well as all the physical demands this character put on them, they also had to give a performance."[23] Ron Mueck was the primary performer on Ludo, developing both his personality and his voice. Rob was his alternate.

"Ludo was a learn-as-you-go project," recalls Connie Peterson. "He was kind of heavy, and we had to lighten him, so we made his thighs—these great big pieces—and his forearms out of Kevlar shells, which were like giant potato chips, very lightweight. The thing that remained heavy was his spine because it had to support an awful lot of stuff, with the foam latex and his hair and everything."

RIGHT Ludo evolves through the magic of Brian Froud's pencil, slowly becoming the creature audiences know and love (top). Studies by John Stevenson explore various Ludo expressions (bottom). **BELOW** Ludo prepares to call the rocks.

1983
Ludo
Brian Froud

"Basically, my dad let [Ron Mueck] do everything," Brian Henson says, "which is very rare. . . . Ron sculpted Ludo. Ron molded Ludo. Ron fabricated Ludo. Ron came up with the whole costume—I call it an exoskeleton. And then Ron performed Ludo as well. His feet were in Ludo's feet. His arms were in Ludo's arms—but his hand probably came to just past Ludo's elbow, and then he had controls there to work the hands, which were farther away."

A three-person team also remotely operated Ludo's animatronic facial features. Francis Wright worked the eyebrows (one lever rotated the eyebrows, and the other moved them up and down); Sue Dacre controlled the eyeballs and eyelids with a joystick; and Don Austen controlled all the lip shapes and movements, precisely lip-syncing to the lines that Ron delivered from within Ludo.

One key area that Mueck was not involved in was the creation of Ludo's hair, which was made of sisal, a natural grasslike material. "It looked right for him, and it was cost-effective," relates Connie Peterson. "Ludo's pelt was created on knitting machines operated by a trio of ladies: Val Jones, Cass Willing, and Lesja Liber. They had done a lot of research and development with those machines, so they took charge. After they knitted the hide from some henna-red wool, they went back and knitted in the sisal fibers."

The shooting schedule did Ludo's team no favors. Peterson explains, "We didn't have a shooting schedule when we started working on the characters. So we didn't know what we were supposed to be starting with. And it turned out that day one or day two of the schedule was the scene where they drop Ludo from the tree [after the goblins torment him]. Well, that meant we had to call in a stuntman so we could show him Ludo and say, 'We have to hang Ludo upside down from a tree, then drop him and have him sit up, all in the same shot. How do we do that without killing the puppeteer?'

"We already had two Ludos for different scenes, but the stuntman said we had to make a third one that was all soft, just for the stunt—so the puppeteer could fall in it and not break his back. The knitting ladies thought they were done after making the coats for two Ludos, but suddenly they were told to knit another one."

LEFT (top to bottom) Didymus, Ambrosius, Sarah, and Ludo enter the Goblin City with Kevin Clash on the floor performing Ambrosius. Puppet builder and performer Ron Mueck rehearses with Ludo's head. Rob Mills takes his turn inside the Ludo costume. Jim Henson's gently assertive directing style was effective with all manner of actors, be they beast or fair maiden.
ABOVE Ludo—or rather, the performer inside him—cools off between takes.

The Junk Lady

"Everything in the world you've ever cared about is all right here."—THE JUNK LADY

PUPPETEER: KAREN PRELL

VOICE: DENISE BRYER

CREATURE SHOP TEAM: WENDY FROUD, SHERRY AMOTT, CHERYL HENSON, MAVIS TAYLOR, GRAEME GALVIN, GINETTE ST. CLAIR RUTHVEN, JASON REED, GEOFF PAIGE, SUSIE CARTER, ALISON DARKE

The Junk Lady that Sarah encounters is a very memorable character, but Connie Peterson says there could have been a lot more junk piled on top of her. "We made a lot of stuff for those scenes that you don't see on the screen," she says. "We had people going to all the antique markets, all the secondhand places—London's full of them—just getting weird, eccentric stuff."

The Junk Lady's overburdened situation is a metaphor for Sarah's confused state of mind following her graceful fall from the ballroom bubble. As the young girl realizes that her precious childhood keepsakes are becoming a similar burden—"It's all junk!" Sarah cries—the audience understands that she's taken a bold step toward maturity.

Like Ludo and Hoggle, the Junk Lady was a wearable puppet creation—with puppeteer Karen Prell positioned inside the bulky costume. She kept her hand inside the puppet's face, while her own face was hidden behind the upside-down chair the Junk Lady carries on her back.

ABOVE A preproduction painting by Brian Froud depicts a very different, almost elegant Junk Lady. **TOP RIGHT** Although Henson asked the Creature Shop to fabricate five different characters for the junk world sequence, he ultimately chose to showcase only one: the Junk Lady, portrayed by puppeteer Karen Prell. **BOTTOM RIGHT** Brian Froud's working sketch bears a strong resemblance to the Junk Lady's final appearance. **FOLLOWING SPREAD** Cinematographer Alex Thomson, seated atop the camera crane, captures Sarah wandering through the expansive junk world set.

"I had a video monitor around my neck so I could watch the camera feed," recalls Prell. "For the era, it was small—about the size of a loaf of bread with the screen at the end of it, hanging around my neck. . . . So it wasn't easy, looking out through the chair just to see where I was going, while checking my position with the camera feed on the monitor."

Prell explains, "When the character had to be very mobile, like out in the junk world, then it was just me in there. But once we were in Sarah's little room set, she had to be handling the props and giving them to Sarah. That's when they put a person on a little rolling cart between my legs, reaching up into both of the Junk Lady's live hands!"

Prell laughs about it today. "So there I was, shuffling through the set with this costume on my back, and a puppeteer between my legs. I was shuffling because that's all the leg movement I was capable of. I think all of this added to the look and the feel of the Junk Lady because, of course, she is supposed to be weighed down by everything. And inside—I certainly was!"

Prell had creative fun with the character and rehearsed specific movements with Toby Philpott, the puppeteer who performed the Junk Lady's face and eye movements via radio control. "Toby controlled her eye turns," Prell says. "I did her brows and her jaw. So I'd tell him, 'Let's do a lot of looks where she's glancing to the sides.' For certain lines, I'd suggest, 'I'm going to have my head this way, looking away from Sarah. But you turn her eyes to look to Sarah, so that it seems like she's behaving surreptitiously, and suspicious of the girl. We tried to get that in there just to show that the Junk Lady wasn't all she seemed."

Brian Henson was in his early twenties when he worked on *Labyrinth*, and he comments that the metaphor of the Junk Lady and her burden didn't quite hit home: "I didn't get it then because I was light as a feather and free as a bird and young and single. But now, at the ripe old age of fifty-two, I'm very aware of what it feels like to be moving through your life with all this baggage on your shoulders all the time!"

The Wiseman (and His Hat)

"Zzzzzzzzzzzzz."—THE WISEMAN

"Ah, it's so stimulating being your hat!"—THE HAT

PUPPETEERS: FRANK OZ (THE WISEMAN) / DAVE GOELZ (THE HAT)

VOICES: MICHAEL HORDERN (THE WISEMAN) / DAVID SHAUGHNESSY (THE HAT)

CREATURE SHOP TEAM: SHERRY AMOTT, ROLLIE KREWSON, RICKY EYRES, IAN ROLPH, RON MUECK, JASON REED, GEOFF PAIGE

The Wiseman didn't have much screen time, despite the splendid piece of concept art—painted by Brian Froud in 1984—that inspired his appearance. His entrance wasn't at all grand: In the film, he simply totters into the frame and seats himself upon a curious throne constructed of oversized "stone" books. The throne was a convenient place to hide the puppet operator once the Wiseman sat down. Comfortably ensconced within the throne, which was open in the back, the primary puppeteer was able to operate the character's main movements while additional puppeteers nearby used radio controls to operate the Wiseman's facial movements.

"He had lots of radio controls built into him," says Krewson. "That was the tricky part of him—making sure everything worked. The puppet had a boned body with clothing on top of that. The head and the bird were one unit, so there was a neck sleeve that went down through the body and the puppeteer performed through there."

Frank Oz, Jim Henson's talented longtime friend and associate, was the primary performer of the Wiseman character. Oz had little time to perform a major role in *Labyrinth* because he was busy directing the movie *Little Shop of Horrors* (1986) in a nearby studio, but he was able to make time to play the Wiseman. "Jim especially asked me to do it," commented Oz at the time. "Maybe it's partly to celebrate the fact that we're about to celebrate our twenty-one years together!"[24]

"He just showed up the day we shot it," recalls Dave Goelz, who played the Hat. "We didn't really have any rehearsal time. We just worked it out on the set: developed the material a little and modified the script a bit to

LEFT Early sketches by Brian Froud show that the Wiseman wore many hats before his look was finalized. **ABOVE** A sketch by Brain Froud of the Wiseman and his Hat.

accommodate the relationship between the two characters—which was a lot like the relationship between Frank and me. He was my mentor all through *The Muppet Show*. I would pester him. I still do. I still pester him as much as possible."

If Goelz had the honor of being the Hat, puppeteer Toby Philpott got to be "Frank's other arm." Philpott was an experienced performer—he had operated the Alchemist in *The Dark Crystal*, and he was one of the three puppeteers who jointly performed Jabba the Hutt in *Star Wars: Episode VI Return of the Jedi* (1983). However, by the time he found out about the production for *Labyrinth*, all the major roles had been cast. Nevertheless, the crew invited Philpott to come aboard as a fill-in puppeteer. He says, "Then they mentioned to me that if I hung around another week, Frank Oz was coming by to play an old man who talks through his hat—and he needed someone to do one of the character's hands."

Sure enough, the next week, Philpott received a summons. Then afterward, Frank Oz, the legendary puppeteer, cast Philpott as one of the principal plant performers (along with Brian Henson and several others from *Labyrinth*) in *Little Shop of Horrors*.

LEFT Close-up of the fully realized Wiseman and Hat shows the detail in workmanship, from the Hat's beady eyes to the realistically aged skin of the Wiseman's hands. **TOP RIGHT** Brian Froud's vivid painting of the Wiseman and his Hat, which in this version appears to be a duck. **BOTTOM RIGHT** Well-known puppeteer Frank Oz primarily performed the Wiseman from this comfortable position within the character's chair. **FOLLOWING SPREAD** For close-up shots of the Wiseman's face, Oz had to assume a more awkward (although not unusual for a puppeteer) position on his back.

The Worm

"Come in and have a nice cup of tea."—THE WORM

PUPPETEER: KAREN PRELL

VOICE: TIMOTHY BATESON

CREATURE SHOP TEAM: GARY POLLARD, MARION APPLETON, IAN ROLPH, TONY DUNSTERVILLE

One of the first inhabitants of the labyrinth that Sarah encounters is a delightfully courteous character known simply as the Worm. Quick to offer a bit of sympathy and "a cuppa" with him and his "missus," the Worm quickly became a fan favorite—a fact that continues to surprise and delight Karen Prell, the little fellow's operator. "The scene with the Worm was such a small part of the schedule compared to all the other big set pieces we were doing," says Prell. "But this is a kind of calm, quiet scene that gives people an appealing introduction as to how characters in the labyrinth work."

Prell was assigned to operate two different versions of the Worm for the scene—a small one for shots with Jennifer Connelly, and a big one for close-ups. "The small worm puppet was totally old school," Prell relates. "It was solid foam rubber with two very, very thin rods going into the head and the tail. That was performed on the set where Jennifer was, and little holes were drilled through the bricks [of the wall] for the rods. We'd switch to the big puppet for the other shots."

That big puppet was quite large—perhaps three feet long, Prell says, "if it had been all stretched out—but it was operated in a curved position. I was behind a piece of wall made up of giant-sized bricks so they'd be the right scale for the bigger worm. There was a hole in the belly where the Worm was resting on top of the bricks. The hole was large enough for me to reach up inside, and for another puppeteer to reach up and operate the tail from inside—just to give it a little bit of movement."

Prell continues, "My right hand was reaching through the wall into the Worm's head, and my left hand was operating a joystick while I was looking at a monitor with the camera feed. So I operated my own controls for the eye turns and eye blinks. Normally, that doesn't happen. Typically, when you're performing a puppet, your nonpuppeteering hand is tied up with other things. But because this was a stationary character with no extra limbs except for its tail, my hand was free to do my own facial expressions. That's very helpful. Otherwise, you have another person—or, in the case of, say, Ludo and Hoggle, several people—perform the face. That requires a lot of rehearsal, with everybody working to get into each other's rhythms. I didn't have to do that for the Worm. I could just sit and operate it and be spontaneous with the performance."

LEFT An early sketch of the character by Brian Froud suggests a creature more closely related to a caterpillar than a worm. **BELOW** "Ello!" Although the Worm was very friendly, he gave Sarah a bit of misdirection that made her quest longer and more perilous.

Humongous

"Where's reverse?"—HOGGLE

SPECIAL EFFECTS SUPERVISER: GEORGE GIBBS

Humongous is the guard at the gates to Goblin City. In fact, he is the gates of Goblin City, each towering door one half of a gigantic warrior in a suit of armor. When Humongous is activated against some perceived threat, the gates slam shut, uniting his two metallic halves. Red eyes aglow, he raises an enormous double-headed ax and steps forward, ready to chop up Jareth's enemies.

At fifteen feet tall, ten feet wide, and approximately two and a half tons, this creation looked more like a robot than a puppet—and it was intimidating, both on camera and off. In fact, Humongous was so intimidating that the Creature Shop didn't even attempt to fabricate him. "We decided to let the special effects department make him," says Brian Henson. "Humongous was so big that we felt he might be dangerous. He was going to be all the things that a special effects department handles routinely—like a bus that can come crashing through a wall and hit the floor without killing all of your actors, because it's been designed to run on rails and hydraulics. . . . The feeling was that Humongous needed that kind of engineering."

George Gibbs was the special effects supervisor for *Labyrinth*, and he came to the production fresh from his Oscar-winning work on *Indiana Jones and the Temple of Doom* (1984). "From drawing board to finished, working creature, Humongous took about five months to make," Gibbs said at the time of the shoot.[25] The creature sprang from a spontaneous idea during preproduction.

ABOVE Brian Froud's sketch of Humongous still incorporated what was then being referred to as the "robot door" that leads to the Goblin City. **RIGHT** Director Jim Henson explains to actress Jennifer Connelly how the robot gatekeeper will wield his axe in the upcoming scene.

"Late in the story," said Jim Henson, "what we wanted was for our heroes to come up against some huge obstacle, something worse than anything they'd encountered so far. And we came up with the idea of building the largest puppet we'd ever built."[25]

"[Jim] said, 'Boys, I'd like a fifteen-foot-high giant,'" recalled Gibbs. "We said, 'Oh, yeah. Very interesting.' Lots of people had tried to make fifteen-foot giants that walk and throw their arms around. They hadn't been very successful. So it was a challenge, really."[27]

"This was the largest, most-complicated thing we'd ever built," Jim Henson said proudly. "When George first showed me Humongous in action, it was really an amazing thing—to just stand there and have this large thing walk toward you. It's one of the most awesome sights in the world."[28]

Though Humongous was extremely impressive and perfectly safe, Shari Weiser, who performed Hoggle, nevertheless was a little horrified when it came time to film the scene where Hoggle bravely leaps onto Humongous's head. "I had a stunt double for the actual jump," Weiser explains, "but I was the one who had to run along the top of the castle wall to get over to where Hoggle makes the jump. And I couldn't see out of Hoggle's head!"

Weiser wore a harness attached to a wire, so she was never in danger of falling. But from inside the Hoggle costume, it felt like she was going to fall—over and over again. "I would run along the wall and as soon as it started that curve, I would run off the wall," she recalls, laughing. "To this day, when I get to the edge of something up high, like a scenic overlook or something, I still panic a little."

LEFT The full-scale puppet of Humongous was as awesome in repose as he was in action. With his great height and tremendous weight, Humongous was almost as scary to the crew as he was to *Labyrinth*'s protagonists.
ABOVE The camera crew captures Humongous's performance for the film.

Chapter Five

"It's All Looking Incredibly Good"

"The Fireys came straight out of Brian Froud's drawings," writer Terry Jones said during filming. "They were obviously sort of wild, you know. And I just imagined that they came in at one point when Sarah was really lost, and they came up with really helpful things. But you're not quite sure how wild they're gonna get! Then they sang a song, saying, 'Lift your feet! Lift your head!' And I thought, 'Ooh! It'd be a good idea if they lifted their heads off their shoulders as they sang that.' Then one would lift his head up and roll it down his shoulders and start tossing it around and playing it like a basketball and lobbing it around."[29]

However, describing the creatures and their antics on paper was one thing. Putting them on screen was another. When choreographer Charles Augins arrived at Elstree Studios to work with the characters, he recalls, "The recording of the song we would be using wasn't finished. They had a working version of this song that David Bowie had written. . . . And the puppets themselves weren't ready yet, either."

"Three puppeteers performed each Firey," says Toby Philpott, who handled the body and legs of Firey #1. "The feet were attached to my feet, and I held the hips and the shoulders of the body from behind. David Barclay was crouched behind me, operating the arms and hands. When I was dancing around, I was trying not to kick him, of course. And Kevin Clash was standing next to me holding the head. It wasn't attached to the body—Kevin was just leaning in and resting the head on the shoulders while we were dancing about together. We invented a lot of the moves that you see in the finished film."

TOP LEFT The inanimate head of Firey #1 is stored on a stand when not in use. Polaroid photo identifies the performer it is assigned to, in this class Kevin Clash. **BOTTOM LEFT** Brian Froud's sketches capture the Fireys' inherent craziness. **RIGHT** Several puppeteers do the work of one Firey.

Philpott says that choreographer Charles Augins "helped us find moves that looked good and worked. He didn't give us steps so much as he offered suggestions about the dynamics of each move."

Augins says, "Jim put me together with Brian Henson and Kevin Clash, the two puppet coordinators for the film, and Cheryl Henson, who built and helped operate one of the Fireys. There were moves I thought couldn't be done, and they'd say, 'Oh yeah, we can do that!' When you're working with bodies, there are limitations. But they taught me that those limitations just did not exist in the world of puppets. Whatever I'd have considered crazy two weeks earlier was normal there. Nobody ever said, 'No, we can't do that.'"

"Once we were into filming, it was so much fun!" says Clash. "A lot of the gags with the bodies coming apart were last-minute additions. But we'd gotten as much figured out as we could in rehearsal because, when we were filming, the performers and the entire set had to be covered in black velvet, so that nothing other than the characters would be picked up by the camera. It was hard to see where we were going. We had to peek at little monitors that were carefully hidden." Afterward, the Fireys, and Jennifer Connelly as Sarah, were composited onto a forest background.

"Velvet is probably the blackest fabric that you can use," Jim Henson said at the time. "We had to get rid of anything reflective. Any little white dots or anything like that would show up. We shot the puppets first with a computerized camera and then we removed the black velvet and shot the background using the computer to make the camera move at exactly the same speed and so forth. Then all these elements were put together later in the laboratory."[30]

Unfortunately, the technique had some drawbacks. "The final Fireys look kind of translucent," says Brian. "The compositing sequence was a complex optical-effect technique that didn't really work. I've often been tempted to go back in and redo that whole sequence. But I don't know if that's a good idea because the film is what the film is. So sometimes they're a little translucent—well, they're fire characters!"

Shafted

"The things I like most about *Labyrinth* are not necessarily things I contributed," writer Terry Jones said. "But the part where Sarah goes down the Shaft of Hands—that was mine." The shaft filled with "helping hands" began as a thirty-foot-tall plywood column—essentially an open-sided tube—designed by special effects supervisor George Gibbs. The interior of the column was covered with foam rubber sculpted to look like a drippy rocky surface. The only problem was that Gibbs's team couldn't apply foam until holes were cut in the plywood for the puppeteers' arms to reach through. And they couldn't cut the holes until the puppeteer teams knew how to position their arms in order to make facial shapes with their hands. And to determine that, the puppeteers had to decide which faces they would make. It was a time-consuming puzzle.

"We were put together as teams of two and three," puppeteer Toby Philpott says. "Jim asked us to improvise ways of making a face with just our bare hands. We did that for a morning, and then after lunch we showed each other what we had. . . . Then we picked the best ones and learned the lines that they'd deliver." When the configurations were chosen, the holes cut, and the foam applied, 200 dummy hands—dark green gloves filled with foam—were attached to the upper portion of the column. Then slits were cut in the foam so that 150 human hands, from 75 humans, could reach through.

LEFT Alex Thomson moves in for a close-up of Firey #4, performed by Steve Whitmire. **ABOVE** Jennifer Connelly appears quite comfortable amid a sea of latex hands.

When filming began, the puppeteers were positioned on five levels of scaffolding, rigged with different places for people to stand, sit, or lie. "Everybody had to climb up ladders on the back of the structure," says Cheryl Henson. "It was set up like bunk beds up there—really tightly packed, barracks-style bunk beds. It looked like little shelves of people. We had to stick our hands into these green, slimy-feeling gloves, and basically just stay there all day."

On the camera side of the column, Connelly found herself in an entirely different situation. Philpott says she "was sitting in a chairlift that went up and down. And the camera was mounted on a forty-foot vertical track that started above Jennifer and followed her descent down the shaft."

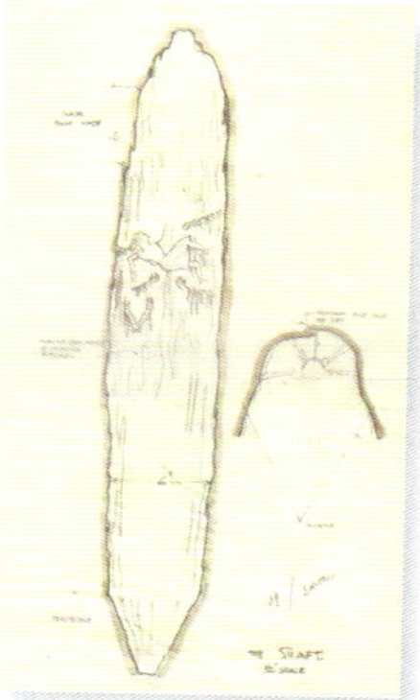

Connelly doesn't recall being scared during the Shaft of Hands sequence—or during any of the other scenes where Sarah was in peril. "It was really fun," she says. "I remember having a great time. People were careful with me, and it was an incredible experience!"

Bogged Down

Labyrinth follows the progress of a teenage girl on the cusp of adulthood—yet the story abounds in scenes aimed at younger children, and at boys in particular. Take, for instance, the Bog of Eternal Stench. What could be more entertaining to young viewers than hearing Ludo complain, "Smell baaad!" amid the familiar, foul toots being emitted by the bubbling Bog?

To create the gaseous sound effects needed for the Bog of Eternal Stench, Jim Henson turned to *Labyrinth* soundtrack composer Trevor Jones. "Jim wanted an assortment of various fart sounds," relates Jones. For *Labyrinth*, Jones performed what were termed "music FX cues" on a Synclavier, an early synthesizer, sampling system, and music workstation. Though Jones's fart noises were certainly comical, the Bog wasn't always a source of amusement for the filmmakers.

ABOVE A conceptual sketch of the Shaft of Hands set provides views of the construction from the side and from above. **BOTTOM LEFT** This behind-the-scenes shot reveals the complexity of the Shaft of Hands set piece. **TOP RIGHT** Elliot Scott's drawing of Hoggle and Sarah standing on a ledge above the Bog of Eternal Stench. **BOTTOM RIGHT** Brian and Jim Henson discuss blocking the next scene with Ludo (played by either Ron Mueck or Rob Mills), Hoggle (Shari Weiser), Sarah (Jennifer Connelly), and choreographer Cheryl Gates McFadden (far right).

"The Bog of Stench really started to smell like the Bog of Stench," recalls puppeteer Kevin Clash. "The special effects people oozed a lot of liquid into the moat of that set. And they never drained it while we were shooting. So it was pretty rank at one point."

After production designer Elliot Scott built the set over a huge tank, he handed the task of filling it to the special effects department. "The Bog had to appear really uninviting, as you can imagine," special effects supervisor George Gibbs added. Gibbs's crew started by filling the tank with thirty thousand gallons of water. "Then we mixed in a ton of something called Celacol, a nontoxic, medium-viscosity jellyfier," Gibbs explained. Celacol is also used in wallpaper paste, shampoos, and countless cosmetic items. To this, he said, "we added brown and blue soluble dyes, plus industrial liquid paraffin for the surface, and also lots of microballoons [like tiny glass beads] to prevent the different-colored dyes and oils from integrating. The result was a nice, gluggy, flexible sludge. But I'm afraid that it became a bit spoiled when people had to wade through it to arrange lights and so on."[31]

Brian Henson's most vivid memory of the Bog of Eternal Stench may be one unfortunate crew member's least-favorite memory. "The tank had a deep area where the rocks rose up in response to Ludo's call," he says. "Most of the Bog was about eighteen inches deep. But the section with the rocks was about eight feet deep. We marked off the edge of the deep section with lots of chains and chain tackles hanging down, so that people would see it.

"We were using Panavision cameras. They were really expensive, a couple hundred thousand dollars each. The first assistant cameraman was the only person allowed to carry those cameras around because they were so valuable. Well, one day he was walking with a camera, and I saw him inadvertently step right into the deep end. He held the camera in one hand, and he grabbed hold of a hanging chain tackle with the other hand. But the chain tackle was all oily from the Bog of Stench. He slowly slid down the chain—and as he slid, he lifted the camera higher with his other hand. He was all the way in by the time somebody was able to get to him and grab the camera. The camera did not go into the Bog!"

Henson chuckles at the memory. "He was in over his head, but he saved the camera. It was pretty impressive."

Ballroom in a Bubble

In 1985, Jim Henson said the ballroom scene "is just about the only crowd scene in the movie where there are only people. There's no puppets there. So it was pretty straightforward to shoot, and we all had a lot of fun doing it."[32]

"The ballroom really was meant to be within a bubble," explained production designer Elliot Scott. "So rather than build a straightforward ballroom, I tried to put together the essence of a ballroom. That is to say, a ballroom to me means columns. So we didn't build columns—we had huge caps [decorative column tops]. It means chandeliers, so we devised massive chandeliers. And there were mirrors, so you saw mirrors and reflections of mirrors in mirrors and things like that."[33]

Scott—who worked with his two art directors, Roger Cain and Peter Howitt, and his son, assistant art director Stephen Scott—planned the set meticulously. He designed the ornate chandeliers, for example, to rotate very slowly, in groups of four, over a ten- to twelve- foot radius. Each of them held at least a dozen foot-high candles that would burn with a naked flame for precisely four and a half hours. Timing was critical. Every hour, a group of the chandeliers arrived in a preplanned position, enabling Scott's crew to change the candles, adjust them, and clean up any spilled wax. Each chandelier was also decorated with long strings of glass teardrop-shaped beads.

PREVIOUS SPREAD Shari Weiser (as Hoggle) and Jennifer Connelly (Sarah) filming the "Bog of Eternal Stench" sequence. **LEFT** Special effects crew members pour bags of Celacol into the artificial bog to create a goopy effect. **TOP RIGHT** Dress sketch by Brian Froud. **BOTTOM RIGHT** Jim Henson shares his vision of the ballroom scenes with a receptive Jennifer Connelly.

Before shooting began, director of photography Alex Thomson needed some help in creating the eerie, dreamlike look of the scene. George Gibbs and his special effects team came to the rescue, creating a "bubble lens" for the cinematographer. The custom-made accessory—manufactured by heating two clear acrylic resin domes to create a slight distortion—was affixed to the camera lens on a small mechanism that rotated as Thomson was shooting. The dreamy effect enhanced the movement of the dancers as they swirled about the room in their elegant couture. Elliot Scott described the dancers' costumes, which Brian Froud and Ellis Flyte created, as "vaguely eighteenth-century Venetian-ballroom-like things with distorted masks. The people in the ballroom were meant to be vaguely depraved, as it were."[34]

"I worked with a team on all of the costumes, male and female, which were cut and stitched to perfection," says Flyte. "Then we weathered and aged them, with eroded hemlines to give the illusion that the costume ball had gone on forever. We even gave the characters broken jewelry."

PREVIOUS SPREAD (top and bottom) Elliot Scott's fascinating set design reflects the "essence of a ballroom," with decorative column tops, candle-laden chandeliers, and a cushion filled lounging area; David Bowie and Jim Henson share a moment between takes on the ballroom set. **LEFT AND TOP RIGHT** Jennifer Connelly and David Bowie pose for a publicity shot—and then just for fun—on the ballroom set. **BOTTOM RIGHT** "Some scenes were done in two takes, others took longer," Connelly said in 1985. "Usually, the ones that took more time were the very technical ones—they require more coordination."

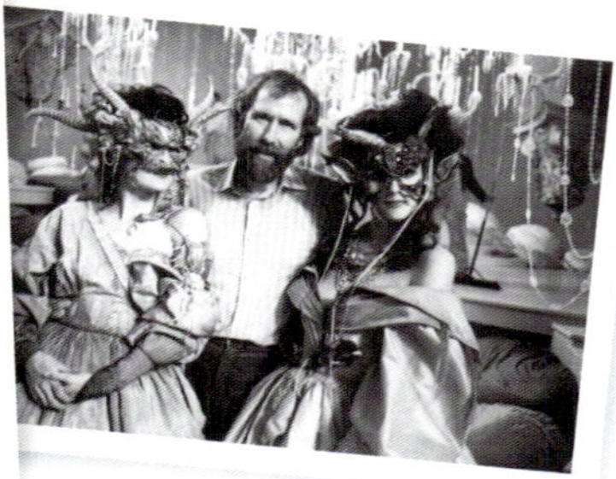

Froud enjoyed the exercise. "I found designing costumes for a bubble an interesting problem," he says. "They were gentry, dressing up and playing at being goblins. And I tried to reflect that in the masks I designed. Although they had this Venetian influence, they're supposed to be parodies of the goblins themselves. I wanted everything much larger than life, as it was a fantasy."

It's hard to miss the Goblin King in the ballroom sequence. He stands out in the crowd, and with good reason. "We embroidered David's blue-black-silver-shot velvet tailcoat with broken jewels and mirrors over the shoulders and front," Flyte notes. "Underneath, he wore an uber jabot shirt [with an extreme ornamental ruffle] in silver silk satin and tight black leggings, overprinted with a subtle silver snakeskin print. And long boots." But in spite of the wanton attention he draws on the dance floor, Jareth has eyes for only one person in the bubble.

"We were trying to create kind of an adult world," revealed Jim Henson. "Sarah is still a child and she's walking into a very adult situation where she knows she's too young to be there. It's something that's attractive to her and it's also repelling."[35]

Wendy Froud comments, "I think that, at some point, it is every young girl's fantasy to go to a different world, meet great characters, and have this great love interest who's so far beyond what you could ever, ever have—or ever want—because he's so much older. That happens for Sarah in the ballroom scene. But the filmmakers were very careful to make it innocent because Sarah is innocent. That's very important. It was a safe way to show a very fun fantasy with great music. And who wouldn't want to dance with David Bowie?"

ABOVE The mask worn by this background dancer is an example of the more revealing cut-out patterns that distinguish Cheryl Henson's designs. Director Jim Henson poses with daughter Cheryl (left) and a costumed dancer. **RIGHT** Wardrobe sketches by Brian Froud reflect the decadent lifestyle of the Goblin Kingdom's glitterati.

Decades later, Connelly still remembers the dress she wore: a billowing silver-white ball gown of iridescent fabric, with puffed sleeves, a silver lace bodice, and a pannier, or hooped petticoat, beneath the skirt. "We made her dress out of silver lamé and iridescent rainbow paper, overlaid with lace and jewels on the bodice," recalls Ellis Flyte. "It all took a great deal of work, but she did look otherworldly!"

"Oh, that enormous hair!" Connelly gasps today. "Who can forget that?" The hairdressers opted not to give her an elegant updo; instead they wove delicate tendrils of silver through her dark hair, like enchanted spiderwebs. She looked older and more mature than a fourteen-year-old—yet younger and far more innocent than the other guests at the ball. "It was such a nice change from the blue jeans that I wore in almost every other scene," she says. "It was really fun at the time. I'd never had an experience like that before, where I'd been dressed like that. It was kind of magical."

Going into Battle with Goblins

"A film like [*Labyrinth*] sort of needs a major climax," Jim Henson said. "And one of the best major climaxes is a battle scene. So we wanted to do a great battle scene. But at the same time, we didn't want to end up killing a lot of people. We didn't want a big gory battle where people got their heads chopped off and things like that. So we were looking [to] have the fun of a battle . . . without being terribly violent. So we decided to do a silly battle."[36]

"My dad was very aware of the fact that children would be watching anything he did," says Cheryl Henson. "That meant keeping the battle really light, and specifically keeping the characters from killing each other. He did not want to show death." Even a goblin apparently squashed by a giant boulder in the battle, notes Cheryl, is lively enough to comment, "Hey—no problem!" afterward.

Trevor Jones's score for the sequence carefully reflected that balance. He says, "It was intended to drive the action, and join the various sections of the battle in one cohesive piece, avoiding treading on the visual jokes and comedic lines, while at the same time giving it a sense of urgency."

TOP LEFT Battle-ready goblins. **BOTTOM LEFT** The goblin cavalry, sans helmets, rehearses. **RIGHT** A riding goblin in the courtyard of the labyrinth. The elaborate costumes were the favorites of many on the set.

Sarah's quest throughout the movie is to rescue baby Toby from the Goblin King. It only made sense that Jareth's goblin minions would participate in the final battle—his many, many goblin minions. Thankfully, Brian Froud already had a book filled with sketches of goblins, and by coincidence or sheer luck, Froud had dressed his creations in armor, with the majority of them carrying weapons. All that had to be done was build them. "Building the creatures in a way that you would believe in them involved a lot of trial and error and subsequent rebuilding to get them right," Froud says. "We used a lot of animated masks worn by actors in a costume."

The question arose: Which of the warriors would be portrayed by costumed actors, and which would be radio-controlled or handheld puppets? "We decided by scale," Froud notes. "We knew we wanted a mix of little and big goblins throughout the movie, and it was easier to cast real people as the larger ones. So when we built prototypes, we started small. But Jim would say, 'Let's have some more of that,' so we'd make them bigger. He always wanted 'more,' as in 'more exciting,' or 'more dangerous.' It was always more, never less, with Jim."

While the Creature Shop was busy building an army, production designer Elliot Scott was constructing a battlefield in the middle of a goblin city. "The Goblin City set was extraordinary," Brian Henson says. "I think the most impressive moment for everyone during the entire *Labyrinth* film shoot was on the morning we first walked onto the Goblin City set."

To enclose the mammoth set, Elliot Scott created what was, at the time, the biggest panoramic backdrop ever made. The lightweight drapery cloth was painted with wispy pink and gray streaks to represent thin clouds filling the sky, and it was hung around the goblin village like a curtain.

Then Scott and his team of craftspeople built a network of narrow cobbled streets and small squares, lined with tiny gabled cottages and houses that tottered and lurched as though designed by a slightly soused goblin architect. At Jim Henson's request, arrangements were made for chickens, pigs, cats, and other animals to wander through the twisting streets. "The whole effect," Scott said during filming, "is that of a fairyland city, conquered some time ago by invading goblins and allowed to go to seed."

Soon, with cameras rolling, the battle was on. As Sarah, Ludo, Hoggle, and Sir Didymus defend themselves, the large goblin army attack. "It was all hands on deck," says Toby Philpott. "Every puppeteer on staff was there. Some of us were up on the battlements, others inside the houses. Jim tried to position as many of us as possible for each shot."

Perhaps the most surprising part of the battle came through the seemingly magical ability that Ludo—and special effects supervisor George Gibbs—share: bringing rocks to life. During the battle, Ludo bellows for help. In response, one hundred boulders of various sizes come tumbling through the city gates

ABOVE Concept artist Elliot Scott's renderings of the Goblin City gates. **TOP RIGHT** In a father-and-son moment, Brian and Jim Henson operate two of their favorite goblins. **BOTTOM RIGHT** (left to right) Henson instructs the brave goblin who will stand at the head of the bowling pin formation of warriors. A goblin and puppeteet rehearsal.

and streets, knocking down the panicked goblins. For the scene, Gibbs made a hundred polyurethane rocks of various sizes, ranging from nine inches to over three feet in diameter.

"We controlled the rocks lots of different ways," Brian Henson says. "Sometimes we put a long rod through a bunch of them, so you could roll them like a giant rake. Others were radio-controlled. And sometimes we just planned out a route for them and let the slope of the road and gravity make it work."

The idea of getting rocks to roll downhill might not sound all that exciting, but Jim Henson disagreed. "He delighted in simple movements that are entertaining," Brian Henson says. "Whenever my dad was producing or directing, he would come in and do a little bit of puppeteering. And always, he'd pick the silliest puppet—like a tiny rod puppet that does nothing but bounce up and down. He loved that sort of thing. But he was too busy directing all the action in the battle to operate one of the puppets. And that is a shame."

How You Turn My World

Finding her way into the center of the labyrinth and into Jareth's castle didn't mean Sarah had reached the end of her journey. Once inside, instead of tangled paths and endless corridors, she faced seemingly endless staircases and the potential entanglement of captive romance. Nothing could be trusted, not even gravity.

As a fan of the math-oriented art of graphic artist M. C. Escher, Jim Henson knew exactly how to bring this aspect of the script to life. Henson asked his production designer, Elliot Scott, to reproduce the artist's multiple-staircased, optical-illusion-inspired piece *Relativity*, so that he could put David Bowie, Jennifer Connelly, and the baby, Toby Froud, inside the set.

"For a graphic artist, creating a two-dimensional optical illusion is difficult enough. But creating it in three dimensions was a real challenge for our production designer," Henson said during filming of the sequence.[37]

"When Scotty was designing the Escher set, he couldn't follow the logic further than two of those odd staircases," notes art director Terry Ackland-Snow. "Well, I made a model, and when I got to about the third staircase, I got lost, too! We made a lot of models, and it took about six weeks to kind of work it out. Then one day in the art department, a mirror fell off the wall and landed on one of the models. Suddenly, we could see the model from different angles, and we realized that it was the answer to one of our problems. So we incorporated two large mirrors, about four by six [feet], and they did the trick."

LEFT A view of the Escher-inspired set. **ABOVE** Henson and Connelly stand on the ledge from which Sarah will make her leap of faith.

The set, once it was built, "was about forty feet high," Ackland-Snow says. At that point, Jim Henson was able to walk through it and carefully plan his shots. "We very carefully storyboarded this whole sequence and followed it closer than we ever did anywhere else in the film," Henson said. "Because there were sequences in here where we wanted David to do things that you couldn't really do."[38]

A few years later, they probably could have created the sequence with computer graphics, but not in 1985. "We shot the Escher sequence on the set," Brian Henson says. "When you walked onto the stage, you couldn't see the entire set as a structure." This was because the various staircases appeared attached to one another only when observed from a certain angle. "We also

LEFT TOP Sarah (Jennifer Connelly) and Toby (Toby Froud) in the center of the labyrinth. **LEFT BOTTOM** Jareth presides over the beautiful Escher-inspired set as the adventure nears its climax. **RIGHT** As the camera rolls, Jennifer Connelly leaps onto a stunt pad while stunt professionals stand by to assist.

shot some split-screen opticals," Brian adds, "like when Sarah is walking on the top of a ledge and Jareth is walking, seemingly upside down, below her." To create the split screen, the scene was shot with Jennifer Connelly walking on a surface, then a similar shot was filmed with David Bowie. In postproduction, the matching shots were composited together, with the Bowie images flipped upside down.

Escher's image creates "gravity wells." Unlike in real life, gravity seems to flow in different directions as people within the drawing walk on different sides of the same surface or have different orientations within the same room. That's the essence Jim Henson wished to capture. Brian says, "My dad worked out very complicated shots that allowed the gravity to flow differently in different sections. One trick we had was using a puppet of Toby. That way, Toby could be on a different gravity plane than Sarah because we had a puppeteer in the ceiling working the Toby puppet by reaching down through an upside-down staircase. Toby could sit on any surface and appear to be using a completely different gravity source."

"Scotty designed [that set] so there's nothing that tells you what's up or down," Jim Henson commented. "And everything intercuts. In other words, it's all lit so that there's no giveaway as to what's top and what's bottom, which means you can never orient yourself to what you're looking at."[39]

Chapter Six

What Kind of Magic Spell to Use

Following their initial conversations about *Labyrinth*, composer Trevor Jones and Jim Henson stayed in close touch. "We agreed," says Jones, "that David [Bowie] would write and record the featured songs while I would provide the remainder of the dramatic underscore."

"I remember that some time had passed and my dad hadn't heard anything yet," Brian Henson says. "He was waiting for some demo tracks from David. And then David came in and played him finished tracks that he had recorded with a Harlem choir. My dad had been expecting maybe some piano with David singing along, and here were these gorgeous, virtually finished tracks."[40]

Once he'd heard Bowie's songs, Jones got down to the business of writing the underscore, which he wanted to be organically related to Bowie's music. "I was always conscious that the sounds I was using, though not identical, were from the same family of sounds that David used," he says. "My score was performed on the Synclavier, along with sampled Bowie songs. I never used an orchestra, just the Synclavier, and a saxophone and trumpet on some cues."

ABOVE David Bowie sings "Magic Dance." "There was so much going on in the 'Magic Dance' scene," recalls puppeteer Kevin Clash. "Jim [Henson] wanted a master shot where we saw everything happening. So we had little people on pullies. We had puppets. We had the baby. We had chickens. And there was a real pig that kept falling asleep. It was crazy!" **RIGHT TOP** Choreographer Charles Augins shows Jennifer Connelly some Firey moves. **RIGHT BOTTOM** Surrounded by black velvet, Jennifer Connelly interacts with the Fireys.

"I loved what [Bowie] did," Jim Henson explained. "As we worked on developing the story of *Labyrinth*, there were several places where music seemed logical. We would talk to David about them. The music and songs he wrote surprised me. He was always doing interesting things musically."[41] David Bowie wrote five songs in total for *Labyrinth*. "Jim gave me a complete free hand," he said. "He allowed me to say what I wanted, write the things that I wanted."[42]

First was "Chilly Down," the only song in the movie that Bowie wrote but didn't sing. Bowie referred to the song as "a little swamp-type number for . . . the Fireys."[43] Sarah meets the Fireys at a vulnerable moment in her journey: She's lost track of her friends and is lost in the woods. She's understandably stressed—even more so after these kooky birdlike creatures jump out of the trees and tell her to relax and chill out, or as they put it, "chilly down."

Along with the song's choreographer, Charles Augins, "Chilly Down" features dancer Danny John-Jules, dancer Richard Bodkin (who also danced in Bowie's 1986 movie *Absolute Beginners*), and puppeteer Kevin Clash. "We prerecorded all the songs before shooting the scene," Clash says. "I had a great time—but I had to keep pinching myself because I never thought that I would be singing at Abbey Road Studios, where the Beatles once recorded!"

The song "Underground" is heard twice in the movie, initially as a soft, choir-free version played over the opening credits, and later as the longer, louder, edgier version heard over the end credits. Bowie's lyrics, "No one can blame you / For walking away / Too much rejection / No love injection"—seem to summarize the emotions that motivated Sarah to give away her baby brother. But even though the lyrics sound as though her journey will lead her to something, or someone, worthy of her ("You'll find someone true / Down in the underground / A land serene / A crystal moon"), they also promise, rather ominously, "It's only forever / Not long at all / Lost and lonely / That's underground," which sounds more funereal than romantic.

The song "Magic Dance" reminds listeners that David Bowie knew how to have a good time—even when surrounded by a plethora of intellectually challenged goblins. It's a simple dance number that's driven by an electric bass and emphatic drums. The opening lines—spoken, rather than sung—are a direct homage to a classic comedic exchange from the 1947 movie *The Bachelor and the Bobby-Soxer.*

LEFT During rehearsal of "Chilly Down," Karen Perell, who performed Firey #2, finds herself in an awkward position. **RIGHT** A rehearsal for the "Magic Dance" sequence.

"['Magic Dance'] gave me a bit of a problem . . . " Bowie said. To perform on the track, he'd picked the child of one of the backing singers, Diva Gray. But "this cute little baby . . . couldn't put two gurgles together. So I ended up doing the baby gurgles. So I'm the baby on that track as well."[43]

In the Escher room scene, "Within You" is a more emotionally powerful song, and it was his "favorite track," Bowie said. "I had to write something that sounded like stone walls and crumbling power. The overall effect, with Jim's visuals, is, I think, very tragic and slightly disturbing."[44] The lyrics suggest that Sarah is far stronger than Jareth anticipated—and it's really vexing him: "How you turned my world, you precious thing / You starve and near exhaust me / Everything I've done, I've done for you / I move the stars for no one."

The mournful repeated line at the end, "I can't live within you," suggests that Jareth acknowledges that he's the byproduct of her childish imagination, which she's on the verge of leaving behind. It's his power over her, real or not, that's crumbling.

It's also Bowie's favorite scene in the film. "It's so sad, I think, because Sarah really likes Jareth," he said, "but she must get her baby brother Toby back safely. So she has to reject all Jareth's pleas for companionship in his lonely world. Jennifer Connelly's performance in this sequence is particularly good."[45]

Perhaps the most beautiful of the songs Bowie wrote for the film is "As the World Falls Down," written for the ballroom scene. Bowie commented, "Jim wanted something which was fairly old-fashioned in its sentiments, and it is, for me, the prettiest tune in the movie and the most relaxed."[47]

It's a straightforward romantic ballad that plays when Sarah is in a poison peach–induced haze, confused and lost. In the film, Jareth reminds Sarah and the audience, "There's such a fooled heart." The emotional turmoil Sarah's experiencing "makes no sense" to her. She isn't ready for the world of her childhood to fall—not quite yet, anyway. So she breaks through the shimmering bubble of adult fantasy that surrounds her.

When *Labyrinth* was released, Jim Henson said of the film's music: "Trevor's score was for the most part inspired by the melody of David's songs. There was practically a fusion between the two, the songs—which we didn't touch—and the score, which accompanies the songs and focuses on them. The songs and the score needed to create a general harmony, and I was very satisfied with the result."[48]

RIGHT Prepping the throne room for "Magic Dance."

Chapter Seven

Everything That You Wanted, I Have Done

"Back in the days when *Labyrinth* was being made, big movies didn't happen in post," says Brian Henson. "In those days, big movies all happened in preparation. So you would preproduce a movie for a year—you would storyboard it, and there'd be eight different versions of every set, so you could pull off every shot." And because Jim Henson had done nearly all the tricky effects scenes live on the set, the postproduction period between the final footage and the final film consisted mainly of editing. Henson annotated the initial shot number for each scene. For example, the oubliette scene, when Sarah falls into the hole, began with shot number 158 and ran through number 165, which indicated the sequence had eight different camera setups. The eighth notes mark the film's music sequences.

There was, however, a lot of film to edit.

On September 6, 1985, after twenty-one weeks of principal photography, the cameras finally stopped rolling, and it was time to start the editing process in earnest. Jim sat down in London to assemble the footage with the film's editor, John Grover. They completed the first cut by October 17, and a week later, Jim turned it over to George Lucas. "I did the first cut," Jim explained, "and then George got heavily involved on bringing it [close] to the final cut."[49]

"Being an editor," Lucas explains, "and having come through that side of the business, just being able to get with the material and work with it and see what I can do is always valuable for me in understanding some of the issues that are involved, either positive or negative. In *Labyrinth*, I moved some things around—sequences—and generally did an edit on the movie."

BELOW Executive producer George Lucas (right) visits Henson on the soundstage during filming. **RIGHT** On the inside cover of his copy of the script, Jim Henson annotated the initial shot number for each scene.

"After that, I took it over again," Jim said. "When you edit a film with somebody else, you have to compromise. George tends to be very action-oriented, and he cuts dialogue quite tight. I tend to cut looser and go for more lyrical pauses, which can slow the story. So I loosen up his tightness, and he tightens up my looseness."[50]

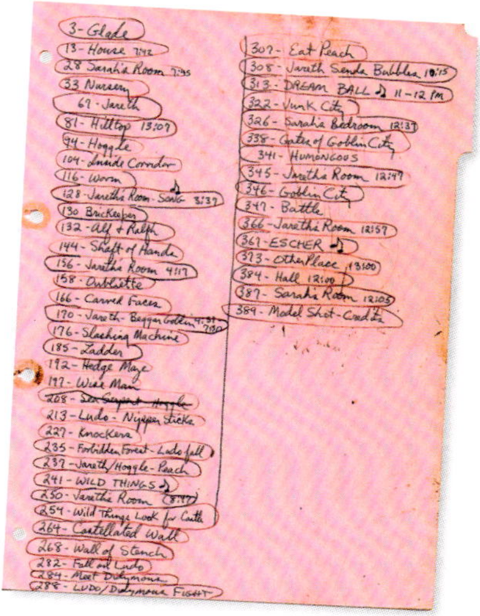
3 - Glade
13 - House 7:42
28 Sarah's Room 7:35
33 Nursery
67 - Jareth
81 - Hilltop 13:07
94 - Hoggle
104 - Inside Corridor
116 - Worm
128 - Jareth's Room - Song 3:37
130 Brickkeeper
132 - Alf + Ralph
144 - Shaft of Hands
156 - Jareth's Room 4:17
158 - Oubliette
166 - Carved Faces
170 - Jareth - Beggar Goblin 4:31 7:30
176 - Slashing Machine
185 - Ladder
192 - Hedge Maze
197 - Wise Man
208 - [illegible]
213 - Ludo - Nipper Sticks
227 - Knockers
235 - Forbidden Forest - Ludo fall
237 - Jareth/Hoggle - Peach
241 - WILD THINGS ♪
250 - Jareth's Room 8:47
254 - Wild Things Look for Castle
264 - Castellated Wall
268 - Wall of Stench
282 - Fall of Ludo
284 - Meet Didymus
288 - LUDO/Didymus FIGHT
307 - Eat Peach
308 - Jareth Sends Bubbles 10:15
313 - DREAM BALL ♪ 11-12 PM
322 - Junk City
326 - Sarah's Bedroom 12:37
338 - Gates of Goblin City
341 - HUMONGOUS
345 - Jareth's Room 12:47
346 - Goblin City
347 - Battle
366 - Jareth's Room 12:57
367 - ESCHER ♪
373 - Other Place 13:00
384 - Hall 12:00
387 - Sarah's Room 12:05
389 - Model Shot - Credits

"I'm strong with script and editing," Lucas told Aljean Harmetz of *The New York Times* in September 1985. "One of the reasons I got involved was that this picture doesn't talk down to kids. I've been involved in one way or another in every story made in this genre for the last five years—*E.T.*, *Return to Oz*, *Dragonslayer*, and my own films. One contribution I could make to *Labyrinth* was to keep the script focused. It's a real trick to keep a script focused, to keep it from going for the amusing incident."[51]

During this same period, Jim also supervised the extensive vocal rerecording sessions. "I had to rerecord almost all of Hoggle's dialogue," says Brian Henson, "because the puppetry controls that I had been operating made clickety-clack sounds. All of the puppets had motors and mechanicals in them that would wipe out the soundtrack. Even Jennifer had to come in and rerecord her dialogue because whenever she was close to the puppets, all of those little motors and clickety-clack sounds covered her lines."

Finally, after Jim Henson had taken another turn in the editing room, a rough cut was deemed ready. In mid-March 1986, a print of the cut was shown in San Francisco, George Lucas's home turf, for a set of sneak screenings.

Two days after the screenings, Jim wrote a memo to his staff: "Both the adult and children's audiences seemed to really enjoy this film, and we are quite pleased with the response. Some scenes need a bit of tweaking and shaping, but happily, no major changes have been called for." The director took special glee in one audience member's comment: "Even though he didn't get the names right, we hope you will all agree with the comments of a young viewer, 'Warthedge and the big ape were really great.'"

Enter the Owl

"We didn't know what the owl in the opening credits was going to look like while we were making the movie," says Brian Henson, "but I knew my dad was really excited about it."

Dennis Lee's novella for *Labyrinth* doesn't mention an owl or a bird of any kind. In Terry Jones's original script, Sarah asks a "white bird" to soar over the labyrinth and tell her what's out there, but a few drafts later, those scenes disappeared. The bird, however, stayed, albeit as part of the opening credits. In Laura Phillips's version of the script, the credit sequence restores the "white bird" and specifies its species:

Blackness.

A hand on which is perched a white barn owl enters the frame.

The white owl stretches its wings and takes to flight in SLOW MOTION.

No mention is made of whose hand is holding the owl, but a character list in the film's early production notes explains that the white owl is "one of the many manifestations of the Goblin King." Regardless, an owl needed to fly over the production credits, and the trick was how to film the creature.

The producers hired an animal trainer and a live owl, but when the trainer released the bird in the soundstage, it flew up to the rafters and wouldn't come down. Next, the Creature Shop built a beautiful puppet owl, but ultimately, it didn't look quite realistic enough to be used during the extended credit sequence. So the puppet was only used in quick shots: the chaotic scene in Toby's bedroom after Sarah realizes he's been taken by goblins; at the window, outside of the bedroom; and in a few shots toward the end of the film, interspersed with quick shots of the real owl.

Then Jim Henson had an idea—one that involved cutting-edge technology. He knew that a Los Angeles–based company called Digital Productions owned a Cray X-MP supercomputer, then the most powerful computer in the world. At the time, it was the only Cray in the world not controlled by the US military, and Digital Productions was experimenting with computer animation.

Thus, in 1986, Jim approached John Whitney Jr. and Gary Demos, the founders of Digital Productions, and proposed creating a realistic computer-animated bird for *Labyrinth*'s title sequence. Nothing like that had ever been done, but "John and Gary were really anxious to push the medium, so they agreed to take on the job," says Bill Kroyer, the animator who worked on the project. "It was a groundbreaking event because the owl has the distinction of being the first photo-real animal ever completely done by a computer. And it worked pretty well, you know?"

The technicians faced several challenges. No one in the computer industry had perfected making stretchable skin for morphing polygonal shapes. Another concern was the massive complexity of rendering the wings of a bird in flight, and an even more daunting problem was the head—a very complex shape. "Nobody had thought of a way to do that," Kroyer notes. "The industry hadn't gotten there yet. So we came up with a really novel approach. First, we did drawings of what we wanted the owl head to look like. . . . [then Disney sculptor Kathy Zielinski] sculpted an owl head maquette about eighteen inches high, sprayed it black, and gave it back to us."

The team placed the sculpted head on a rotating turntable—literally, a record player—and hung a piece of black felt behind it. Next, they coated a 35-millimeter slide with black paint and, using a razor blade, cut a vertical slit down the middle of the slide. "We put that slide in a projector," Kroyer says, "and projected a vertical white line of light onto that black owl head. We rotated the head just a little bit ninety times. And we took a picture each time, so we ended up with ninety squiggly white lines."

LEFT Jim Henson poses with a (momentarily) cooperative barn owl.

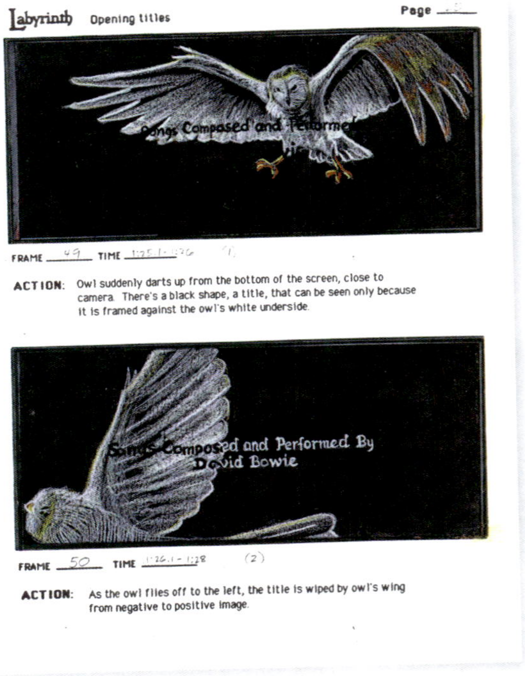

Kroyer continues, "We scanned those ninety lines into the computer, combined them with horizontal lines, and got what looked like a wireframe of the sculpted owl head. Then, we wrote a program to spread that image out. . . . [We] basically unwrapped that three-dimensional thing onto a flat two-dimensional surface. Then we printed that mesh out onto an oversized print, twenty-four by thirty-six inches. We gave that to our matte painter, and he painted in every little detail, the tiny feathers coming out of the eyes, the beak, everything. When we scanned that painting back into the computer and wrapped it around the wireframe, we ended up with the fully textured, photo-real owl head. All of it—the scanning, the true digital mapping—marked the first time that sort of thing had been done."

They weren't done. "Next," Kroyer says, "we built an owl body in the computer. The most difficult thing was to animate the wing flaps. That was insane because an owl has seventeen feathers in his wing and they all move."

To find a model, Kroyer went to LA's Natural History Museum and rented a stuffed owl. He says, "We were able to look

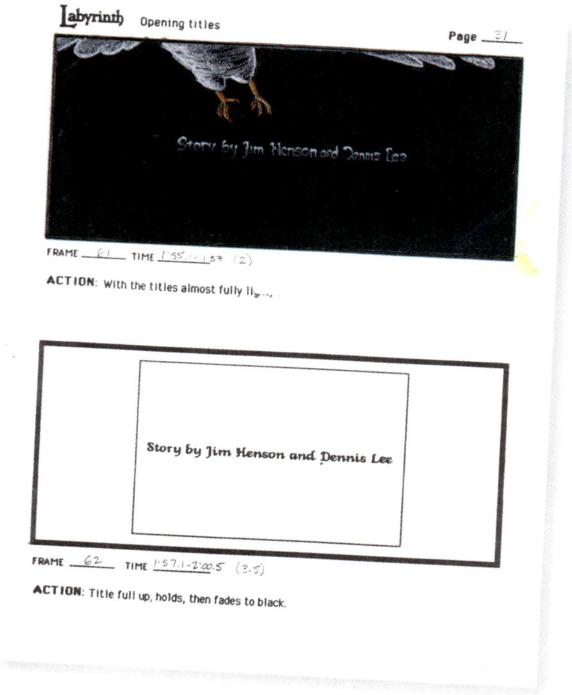

at it very closely and understand how the feathers overlapped. Then we repeated the same thing we'd done with the head. We modeled all seventeen feathers individually as flat polygonal models. That same painter had to paint a feather texture in a completely photorealistic manner. We mapped that onto our seventeen feather wireframes. Luckily, we could just reverse that work for the second wing.

Kroyer explains, "Each of our feather images had to be able to rotate, twist, and bend up and down. I worked on a gigantic monitor. While I worked, behind me, over my shoulder, a 35-millimeter camera stood on a tripod. Every time I set a frame, . . . the camera would take one picture of the screen. To create a five-second test, I would shoot 120 individual frames like that. It took twelve to fourteen hours to complete a few seconds of work. . . . Still, it was incredibly exciting. I'll bet to this day there hasn't been a more accurate wing cycle done in computer graphics."

ABOVE LEFT AND RIGHT A storyboard rendering that helped guide the technicians at Digitial Productions as they created the opening credit sequence.

ABOVE *Labyrinth*'s iconic North American one-sheet poster, rendered by Ted CoConis, who chose to portray Sarah in her beautiful fairy-tale ballgown, rather than the blue jeans she wore in every other scene. **RIGHT** Newspaper reviews of *Labyrinth* from *The Boston Globe*, *New York Daily News*, *The New York Times*, and others.

A Legacy All Its Own

Following some further edits, a bit of sound mixing, and several additional test screenings, the finished film opened at theaters across the United States on June 27, 1986. The reviews were mixed. A number of newspapers, like *The New York Times, The Washington Post,* and *The Boston Globe,* recognized the artistry at work in *Labyrinth*. Nina Darnton of the *Times* stated, "Mr. Henson's creations have put him in the forefront of a development that expands the possibilities of imaginative fantasy that can be transferred to the screen."[52] But other critics were left unmoved, including Roger Ebert and Gene Siskel, the influential hosts of the popular syndicated film review show *At the Movies*. Ebert noted that the film amounted to a lot of creative effort with little payoff, whereas Siskel lambasted Henson for centering the tale on "the sight of a baby in peril."

"We were lost in the crowd," Jim Henson noted. "People thought it was a kids' film. Also, the main character was a young girl, but most of the films that do well in the US have young boys as main characters. And when a boy and a girl want to see different films, they'll compromise by both seeing the one with the boy in it."[53]

However, by the end of 1986, interest in *Labyrinth* wasn't declining but expanding, and the film has since developed a cult following that has extended its life far beyond its initial release. An enduring affection for *Labyrinth* has led to Halloween costumes, activity books, board games, computer games, action figures, plush toys, and even a manga series.

Today, *Labyrinth*'s following continues to grow, making it a strong draw at film festivals and special screenings, and it's a popular component of museum events focusing on Jim Henson's legacy.

The Frouds are likewise frequent guests at fan gatherings around the world, from San Diego's massively attended Comic-Con to other, smaller events. Brian Froud is confident that Henson would be thrilled by the size of *Labyrinth*'s following today. "People thank me for working on the movie," Froud says. "They talk about how the film either got them into the business or turned them on to doing art, or that they got into something else that's creative. And they feel passionate about it. Well, that came straight from Jim. They get that from his vision, and also from his talent for gathering people around him who understood how, through their art, to put that vision into service."

ABOVE Volume One of TokyoPop's manga sequel and Marvel's three-part comic adaptation. **RIGHT** (clockwise from top) One of Bowie's *Labyrinth* 12" single. The front and back cover images from the original *Labyrinth* vinyl soundtrack release in 1986.

Puppet performer Dave Goelz gets a little melancholic when asked how he feels today about the film he worked on almost forty years ago: "I've [watched the film] numerous times, and each time I am utterly touched by it. Because it makes such deep resonant connections with this whole concept of growing up—what do you take forward, and what do you leave behind? Especially at the end, when the characters say to Sarah, 'If you should need us, we'll be there.' It's permission to take childhood forward into life. . . ."

Dave says, "Jim was this businessman who managed to operate this whole big company and get involved with so many enterprises, and at the same time, he was a silly kid. He had this way of functioning fully as an adult and carrying his childhood with him all the time. The movie gives permission to do that. So in a way, it's almost a direct statement of his philosophy. It says, 'You don't have to cross over a line and leave childhood behind and become an adult. You can pick what you take with you.'"

Notes

1. Jim Henson, "Jim Henson's Red Book," Jim Henson Company Archives, quote dated June 27, 1986.

2. Jim Henson, interview with Mary Manilla, Director, Public Relations, Henson Associates, Inc., June 1985.

3. Adam Pirani, "In the 'Labyrinth' with Jim Henson, Part Two," *Starlog*, no. 109 (August 1986).

4. NBC, "Jim Henson," Main Street, April 29, 1986.

5. Henson, interview with Mary Manilla.

6. Brian Jay Jones, *Jim Henson: The Biography* (Ballantine, 2013).

7. Henson, interview with Mary Manilla.

8. Kim "Howard" Johnson, "Terry Jones: Creating the Wonders of *Labyrinth*," *Starlog*, no. 106 (May 1986).

9. Tim Robins, "Labyrinth," *Starburst* (Winter Special 1987/1988).

10. Kim "Howard" Johnson, *Life Before and After Monty Python: The Solo Flights of the Flying Circus* (St. Martin's Press, 1993).

11. Ibid.

12. Pirani, "In the 'Labyrinth' with Jim Henson, Part Two."

13. Jones, *Jim Henson.*

14. Desmond Saunders, dir., *Inside the Labyrinth* (Los Angeles: Jim Henson Television, 1986).

15. *Labyrinth* production notes, TriStar Pictures, 1986.

16. Saunders, *Inside the Labyrinth.*

17. Michael Gillis, dir., *Journey Through the Labyrinth: The Quest for Goblin City*, documentary featurette with "Anniversary Edition" (Los Angeles: Sony Pictures Home Entertainment/Jim Henson Company, 2007).

18. Patrick Daniel O'Neill, "Jennifer Connelly: Growing Up in a World of Fantasy," *Starlog*, no. 108 (July 1986).

19. Michael Gillis, dir., *Journey Through the Labyrinth: Kingdom of Characters*, documentary featurette with "Anniversary Edition" (Los Angeles: Sony Pictures Home Entertainment/Jim Henson Company, 2007).

20. Henson, interview with Mary Manilla.

21. Saunders, *Inside the Labyrinth.*

22. *Labyrinth* production notes.

23. Saunders, *Inside the Labyrinth.*

24. *Labyrinth* production notes.

25. Ibid.

26. Saunders, *Inside the Labyrinth.*

27. Ibid.

28. Ibid.

29. *Labyrinth* production notes.

30. Saunders, *Inside the Labyrinth.*

31. *Labyrinth* production notes.

32. Saunders, *Inside the Labyrinth.*

33. Ibid.

34. Ibid.

35. Ibid.

36. Ibid.

37. Ibid.

38. Ibid.

39. Ibid.

40. Gillis, *Journey Through the Labyrinth: The Quest for Goblin City.*

41. *Labyrinth* production notes.

42. Saunders, *Inside the Labyrinth.*

43. *Labyrinth* production notes.

44. Saunders, *Inside the Labyrinth.*

45. *Labyrinth* production notes.

46. Ibid.

47. Ibid.

48. Alain Schlockoff, "Jim Henson: The Labyrinth Is a Journey," *L'Ecran fantastique,* no. 77 (February 1987).

49. Pirani, "In the 'Labyrinth' with Jim Henson."

50. Ibid.

51. Aljean Harmetz, "*Star Wars* and Muppet Wizards Team Up in *Labyrinth,*" *The New York Times,* September 15, 1985.

52. Nina Darnton, "Jim Henson's *Labyrinth,*" *The New York Times,* June 27, 1986.

53. Schlockoff, "Jim Henson: The Labyrinth Is a Journey."

RIGHT With her Junk lady headgear removed, Karen Prell takes a breather between shots.

INSIGHT EDITIONS
PO Box 3088
San Rafael, CA 94912
www.insighteditions.com

Find us on Facebook: www.facebook.com/InsightEditions
Follow us on Instagram: @insighteditions

™ & © The Jim Henson Company. JIM HENSON'S mark & logo, LABYRINTH mark & logo, characters and elements are trademarks of The Jim Henson Company. Motion Picture © 1986 Labyrinth Enterprises. All Rights Reserved.

All rights reserved. Published by Insight Editions, San Rafael, California, in 2026.

No part of this book may be reproduced in any form without written permission from the publisher.

ISBN: 979-8-3374-0155-3

Publisher: Raoul Goff
SVP, Group Publisher: Vanessa Lopez
VP, Creative: Chrissy Kwasnik
VP, Manufacturing: Alix Nicholaeff
Art Director: Matt Girard
Designer: Allister Fein
Editor: Britny Perilli
Executive Managing Editor: Maria Spano
Senior Production Manager: Greg Steffen
Strategic Production Planner: Lina s Palma-Temena

REPLANTED PAPER

Insight Editions, in association with Roots of Peace, will plant two trees for each tree used in the manufacturing of this book. Roots of Peace is an internationally renowned humanitarian organization dedicated to eradicating land mines worldwide and converting war-torn lands into productive farms and wildlife habitats. Roots of Peace will plant two million fruit and nut trees in Afghanistan and provide farmers there with the skills and support necessary for sustainable land use.

Manufactured in China by Insight Editions

10 9 8 7 6 5 4 3 2 1